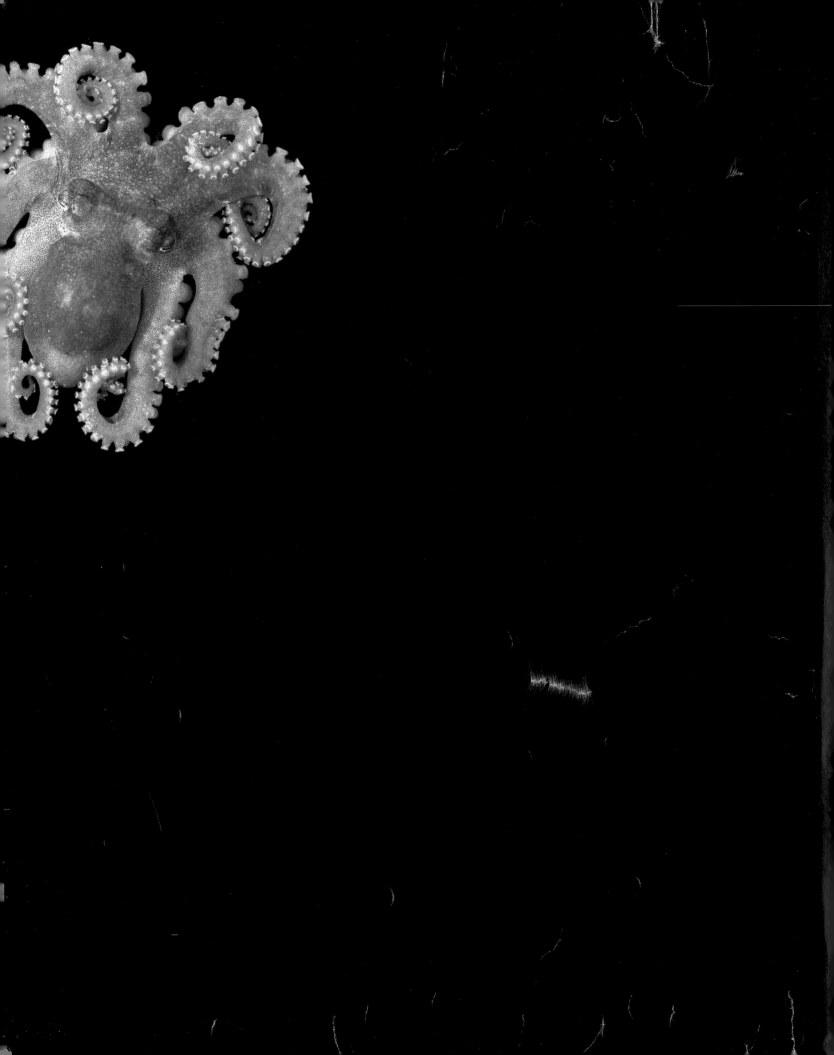

REBECCA L. JOHNSON
FOREWORD BY SYLVIA A. EARLE

journey
INTO THE
deep

discovering
new Ocean
Creatures

M
MILLBROOK PRESS
MINNEAPOLIS

With special thanks to Craig M. Young, who gave me my first opportunity to explore the deep sea in the Johnson-Sea-Link submersible, an incredible experience that changed my life and the way I look at the world
—RLJ

acknowledgments
Part of the delight of writing this book came from talking with scientists involved with the Census of Marine Life (COML) from so many different institutions and countries. All gave generously of their time to answer my questions and describe their experiences. In particular, I'd like to thank Paul Tyler for his encouragement and a friendship that has spanned twenty years, Eva Ramirez-Llodra and Paul Snelgrove for inviting me to COML meetings, and Erik Cordes for his very helpful input. Many thanks also to COML co-senior scientist Ron O'Dor for reviewing the manuscript and to lifelong ocean champion Sylvia Earle for writing the foreword.

Millbrook Press
A division of Lerner Publishing Group, Inc.
241 First Avenue North
Minneapolis, MN 55401 U.S.A.

Website address: www.lernerbooks.com

Library of Congress Cataloging-in-Publication Data

Johnson, Rebecca L.
    Journey into the deep : discovering new ocean creatures / by Rebecca L. Johnson ; with a foreword by Sylvia A. Earle.
        p.   cm.
    Includes bibliographical references and index.
    ISBN: 978–0–7613–4148–2 (lib. bdg. : alk. paper)
    1. Deep-sea animals—Juvenile literature. 2. Deep-sea sounding—Juvenile literature. 3. Deep-sea ecology—Juvenile literature. 4. Scientific expeditions—Juvenile literature. I. Title.
    QL125.5.J64 2011
    591.77—dc22   2009049603

CONTENTS

foreword 4

prologue 5

Shallow edges 8

Open Water 14

deep Slopes 20

cover photo: *This new, yet-to-be-identified type of comb jelly is about the size of an adult thumbprint. Researchers from California's Monterey Bay Aquarium Research Institute discovered and photographed it 6,562 feet (2,000 meters) below the ocean's surface.*

title page photo: *Smaller than a dime, this larva, or very young form, of a bottom-dwelling tube anemone spends the first few months of its life drifting near the ocean's surface.*

contents page photo (top): *A deep-sea Dumbo octopus has webbed arms and fins shaped like elephant ears on its head. Scientists have spotted Dumbo octopuses as deep as 13,123 feet (4,000 meters), often near the seafloor.*

contents page photo (bottom): *The bony "horns" on this tiny yellow boxfish larva discourage other animals from eating it*

the Dark Zone 28

abyssal plains 34

Mountains in the Sea 42

Ridges and Vents 46

the UNFathomable deep 52

epilogue 56

Scientists quoted in this book 60

glossary 61

Source notes 62

Selected bibliography 62

Learn more 63

index 64

foreword

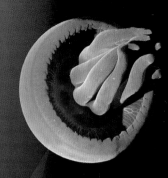

If aliens came looking for life on Earth, they would probably first dive into the sea. This vast blue realm harbors the greatest abundance and diversity of life in the world—or in the universe, as far as anyone knows. Curiously, humans have only recently embarked on serious exploration of the sea. We are just beginning to discover the astonishing variety of creatures who live there. For thousands of years, people traveled over the surface in ships, unaware that the ocean is more than rocks and water. The ocean is alive.

The development of scuba, little submersibles, and other methods for exploring the ocean led to amazing discoveries about the richness of ocean life. Yet far into the twentieth century, many people believed that it was impossible for anything to thrive in the great depths.

A turning point came in 1960 when the bathyscaphe *Trieste* transported two men to the deepest sea, almost 7 miles (11 kilometers) down. As they descended, the pilot, Don Walsh, was surprised to see flashes of bioluminescent light from thousands of small creatures miles below the surface. On the bottom, his companion, Jacques Piccard, saw "a wonderful thing. . . . Just beneath us was some type of flatfish, resembling a sole, about 1 foot [30 centimeters] long and 6 inches [15 centimeters] across. Even as I saw him, his two round eyes on top of his head spied us."

In the years that have followed, it has been confirmed: the ocean is a magnificent, living soup, every spoonful filled with the essence of what makes Earth unique.

Starting in 2000, the Census of Marine Life enlisted teams of scientists from all over the world to more fully explore this "living minestrone" and to answer some seemingly simple questions: How many fish are in the sea? How many kinds of jellyfish, sponges, corals, sea stars, squids, and seaweeds? How do they live? What is the nature of life in the sea at present? What was it like centuries ago? What will it be like centuries from now?

Thousands of new species were encountered, and many more will be found as the samples are analyzed. The most exciting discovery of all may be how much remains to be done. Only about 5 percent of the ocean has been seen so far, let alone explored. Based on what is known of the 250,000 or so species presently accounted for in the sea, there may be 10 or even 50 million more awaiting discovery. Given the diversity of microbial forms, the actual number may approach infinity.

Now we know: among the greatest frontiers for exploration of the universe is the universe of life in the sea, the critically important part of the cosmos that makes our lives possible.

Sylvia A. Earle

ABOVE AND RIGHT: *Big Red jellyfish live at depths of 2,135 to 4,920 feet (about 650 to 1,500 meters). Other jellyfish species use stinging tentacles to catch and kill their food. No one is yet sure how Big Red uses its fleshy arms to feed. In fact, it is so unlike other jellyfish that scientists created a new jellyfish family for it. Its scientific name is Tiburonia granrojo (granrojo is Spanish for "big red").*

Like a spaceship from a distant galaxy, the massive jellyfish hovers in the frigid water. Its meaty dome-shaped bell is as wide as a doorway and the color of a bad bruise. Beneath the bell, fleshy arms twist and sway. The bell contracts, and the jellyfish glides backward. It relaxes, then contracts again. Contract, glide, relax. Contract, glide, relax. With a steady rhythm, the jellyfish pulses through the utter darkness of the deep sea.

Until a few years ago, no one even knew that this species, or kind, of jellyfish existed. The scientists from California's Monterey Bay Aquarium Research Institute who discovered it nicknamed it Big Red. Big Red jellyfish have probably been living in the deep ocean for hundreds of thousands of years. So why hadn't anyone seen one before?

The answer is that even in the twenty-first century, the ocean remains largely unexplored. What we call the Atlantic, Pacific, Indian, Southern, and Arctic oceans are all connected. Together, they form one enormous world ocean that covers about 70 percent of Earth's surface. On average, the ocean is 13,123 feet, or 2.5 miles (4,000 meters) deep. We know less about this huge watery kingdom than we do about many planets in our solar system.

In 2000 scientists from around the world set out on a ten-year quest to learn more about the ocean and everything that lives in it. They called their quest the Census of Marine Life. Several thousand researchers from dozens of countries began the largest ocean exploration in history.

The scientists weren't just looking for new species. They wanted to get a better picture of ocean biodiversity. To do that, they needed to learn more about familiar species as well as any new ones they might find. They also needed to find out which species are common and which ones are rare. Finally, the scientists hoped to discover more about how different species are distributed in the ocean, from the surface to the seafloor and from pole to pole.

"NO ONE'S EVER ATTEMPTED TO DO ANYTHING LIKE THE CENSUS OF MARINE LIFE BEFORE."
—Boris Worm, Dalhousie University, Nova Scotia, Canada

An Antarctic ice fish rests on the seafloor, surrounded by brittle stars. Ice fish can survive in water cold enough to freeze the blood of other fish. Some of the first major scientific expeditions to investigate ocean life around Antarctica took place as part of the Census of Marine Life.

journey iNTO THE deep

How did Census scientists explore something as immense as the ocean? They worked in teams. Different teams studied different parts of the ocean environment. Some teams focused on life in shallow regions. Many others headed into deeper water.

Studying the ocean can be almost as challenging as exploring outer space. You need ships and lots of special equipment. The hours are long, and the work is hard. But you get a chance to be a true explorer. And you never know what you might find.

In these pages, you'll have the chance to explore the ocean alongside teams of scientists working across the globe. You'll visit parts of the ocean few people have ever seen. You'll travel from warm shallow waters to frigid polar seas, from continental edges to deep-sea mountains, and from the ocean's sunlit surface to its deepest, darkest depths. Best of all, you'll get a firsthand look at amazing creatures Census scientists discovered in their quest.

Scientific Classification

Scientists classify, or group, living things based on their similarities. The smallest scientific category is the species. Living things that belong to the same species are very much alike. They can mate and produce offspring. Similar species are grouped together into a larger category called a genus. Together, a living thing's genus name and species name make up its scientific name.

Similar genera (more than one genus) make up a family. Families are grouped to form a class. Several classes make up a phylum, and several phyla together make up a very large, broad category called a kingdom. The Animal Kingdom, for example, includes all the different kinds of animals on Earth.

Discovering a new species is always exciting. During the Census of Marine Life, scientists found thousands of them. They also found several organisms that belong to new genera and new families of living things, such as *Tiburonia granrojo*. That's really rare!

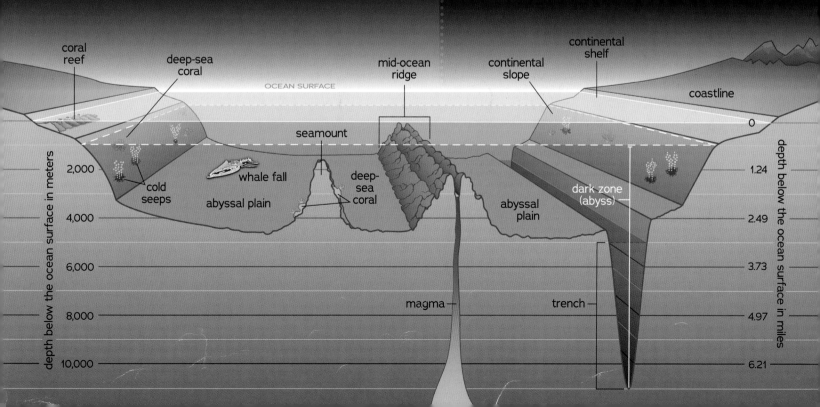

coral reef · deep-sea coral · OCEAN SURFACE · mid-ocean ridge · continental slope · continental shelf · coastline

seamount

whale fall · deep-sea coral · dark zone (abyss)

cold seeps · abyssal plain · abyssal plain

magma · trench

depth below the ocean surface in meters: 2,000 · 4,000 · 6,000 · 8,000 · 10,000

depth below the ocean surface in miles: 0 · 1.24 · 2.49 · 3.73 · 4.97 · 6.21

Shallow edges

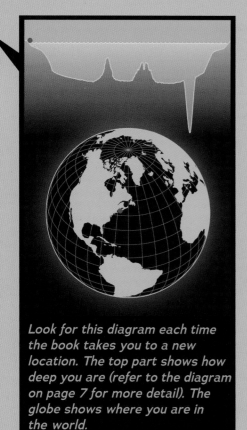

Look for this diagram each time the book takes you to a new location. The top part shows how deep you are (refer to the diagram on page 7 for more detail). The globe shows where you are in the world.

A COLD WIND SWEEPS DOWN MAINE'S RUGGED COAST. WAVES CRASH AGAINST THE ROCKS, SENDING SALT SPRAY HIGH INTO THE AIR. YOU HARDLY NOTICE. YOU ARE FOCUSED ON THE SQUARE FRAME OF PLASTIC PIPE AT YOUR FEET.

Census scientists set out this frame, along with dozens more like it, when the team arrived at this site. They used a global positioning system (GPS) unit to record the exact location of each frame. That's about the most high-tech piece of gear these researchers use, though. The rest of the equipment is pretty simple: rubber boots, buckets, scrapers, these tubular frames, and plastic bags.

You kneel down and peer inside the frame. All the greenish brown bits are algae, or seaweed. They give off a faint stink, like a fish tank that's full of scum. Nestled among the algae are tiny snails . . . and hey! A little crab!

Remembering your instructions, you carefully pick out the animals. The snails—seven of them—go into one plastic bag. The single crab goes into another. Then you scrape all the algae off the rocks and into a bucket. After recording what you've counted and collected in your field notebook, you move on to the next frame.

Back in the laboratory, the scientists will carefully sort through what you and other team members collect. They'll identify the different species of algae and animals. Then they'll put a sample of each species in alcohol. The alcohol keeps the samples from decaying, preserving them for many years.

Preserving organisms means killing them, of course. In the big picture, though, scientists don't

Students from Kyoto University helped Census scientists sample life on rocky shores near the town of Minamisanriku in northern Japan. Here they are counting and collecting snails and other tiny animals inside the plastic frames.

collect and preserve that many living things. They take just enough to create a permanent snapshot of life here along the shore. It's a record that they and other scientists will study for many years to come.

Coastlines are easy to reach and explore in many places. So it's no surprise that coastlines are the most familiar ocean ecosystems. Not until the Census of Marine Life, though, had scientists surveyed and sampled life along coastlines worldwide. They've done surveys like the one you're doing at hundreds of sites on six continents and numerous islands around the globe.

Many of the species they've found are well known. You'd expect that, since people have studied some coasts for centuries. But tucked in among the familiar species are some that are brand new to science.

ABOVE: *This bright yellow kelp, a type of large algae, is a new species from the Aleutian Islands southwest of Alaska. Its leafy blades are nearly 3.3 feet (1 meter) long. Census scientists gave it the name* Aureophycus aleuticus, *which means "golden kelp from the Aleutians."*
BELOW: *Waves pound a rocky stretch of Maine's coastline, where life along the ocean's shallow edges is exposed at low tide.*

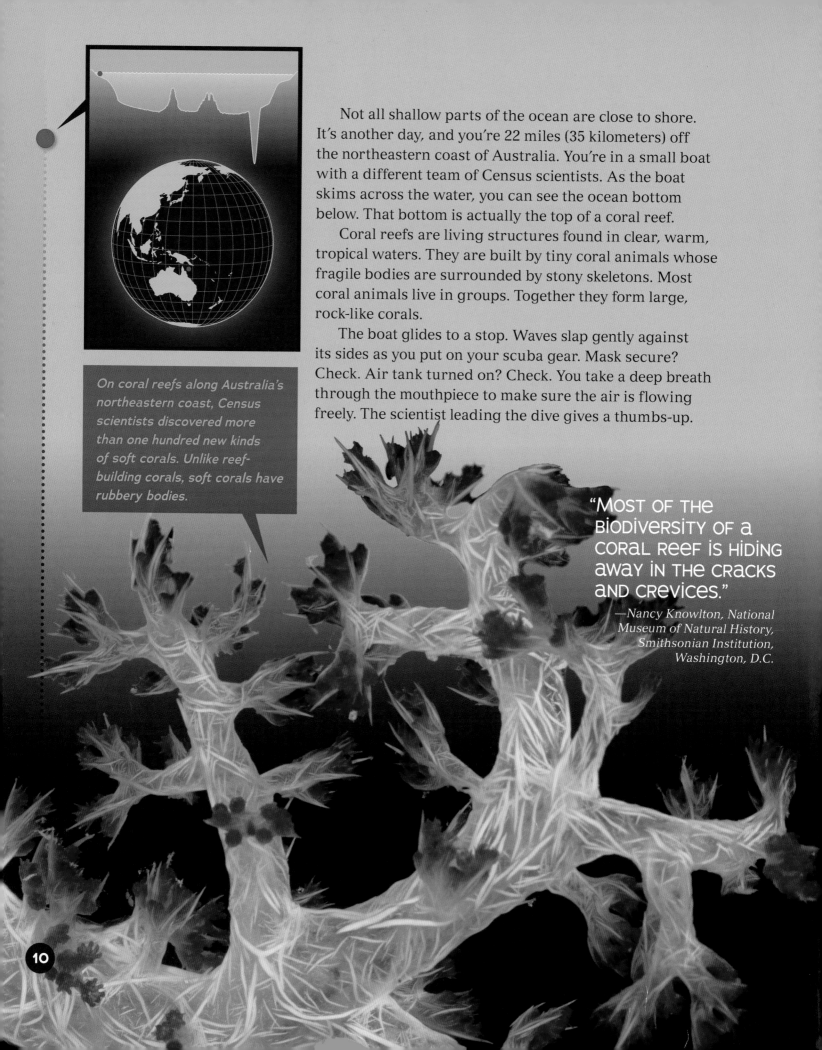

Not all shallow parts of the ocean are close to shore. It's another day, and you're 22 miles (35 kilometers) off the northeastern coast of Australia. You're in a small boat with a different team of Census scientists. As the boat skims across the water, you can see the ocean bottom below. That bottom is actually the top of a coral reef.

Coral reefs are living structures found in clear, warm, tropical waters. They are built by tiny coral animals whose fragile bodies are surrounded by stony skeletons. Most coral animals live in groups. Together they form large, rock-like corals.

The boat glides to a stop. Waves slap gently against its sides as you put on your scuba gear. Mask secure? Check. Air tank turned on? Check. You take a deep breath through the mouthpiece to make sure the air is flowing freely. The scientist leading the dive gives a thumbs-up.

On coral reefs along Australia's northeastern coast, Census scientists discovered more than one hundred new kinds of soft corals. Unlike reef-building corals, soft corals have rubbery bodies.

"MOST OF THE BIODIVERSITY OF a CORAL REEF IS HIDING AWAY IN THE CRACKS AND CREVICES."

—*Nancy Knowlton, National Museum of Natural History, Smithsonian Institution, Washington, D.C.*

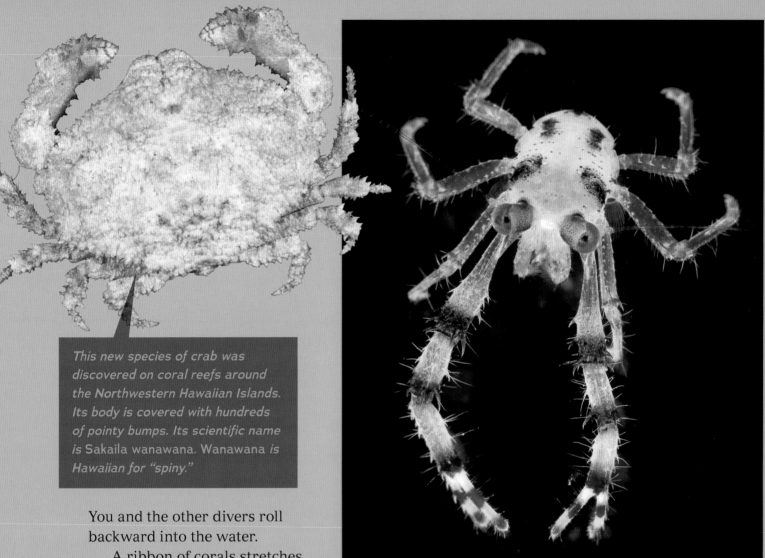

You and the other divers roll backward into the water.

A ribbon of corals stretches out below you. Schools of brightly colored fish swirl past. As you swim over the reef, you spot sponges, sea cucumbers, anemones, spiny sea urchins, and a blue sea star. The reef is jam-packed with life. Scientists think tropical coral reefs might be home to more than one million different kinds of living things.

You head toward a patch of sand between two walls of corals. Small chunks of old, dead coral, called coral heads, lie on the sand. Your job is to pick up several of these coral heads. Another member of the team takes samples of the sand—and whatever lives in it. Two other divers swim over to the walls of living corals to collect tiny reef animals by hand.

After the dive, everyone gathers in the ship's laboratory. One of the scientists uses a hammer and chisel to carefully break apart one of the coral heads. She hands you a tweezers. It takes a long time to pick out everything that's made the coral head its home. You end up with an amazing collection of little worms, snails, shrimps, and crabs.

The scientists use microscopes to examine the animals. Several are types that have never been seen before. The scientists preserve them in alcohol and store them in labeled jars.

ABOVE: *As darkness falls, a scientist uses a light box to see animals on a sandy patch of reef. Many reef creatures are active only at night.*
RIGHT: *Census scientists captured this new species of pygmy octopus on a reef off Australia's northeastern coast. The octopus is small enough to fit in the palm of your hand. The scientists nicknamed it Houdini because it was so good at escaping!*

After sunset the scientists take the small boat out to a sandy patch on the top of the reef. The water here is only knee-deep. You help look for animals that hide during the day but come out at night.

The sand is dotted with slow-moving snails. Suddenly a little octopus slithers past. One of the scientists scoops it into a collecting jar.

Stars glitter overhead as the team heads back to the ship. It would be nice to crawl into your bunk and sleep. But there's still work to be done. In the lab, you help the scientists take tissue samples from the animals that were collected and preserved that day. The bits of tissue are made up of

journey
into the
deep

cells—the building blocks of all living things. The cells contain deoxyribonucleic acid (DNA).

The scientists extract DNA from the cells in each sample. Then they isolate a small piece of that DNA. This tiny piece is called a bar code. The DNA bar code is unique for every species, like a fingerprint.

During the Census, scientists collected DNA bar codes for thousands of ocean organisms. They're building a bar code library for ocean life. When researchers collect something they can't identify, they compare its DNA bar code to those of known species. If there's a match, they know what species they have. If there's no match, it could be something new. Only an expert, though, can determine if an organism is truly a new species. The process involves studying every part of that organism in painstaking detail. That's why it will take years for all the different living things collected during the Census to be classified and given proper scientific names.

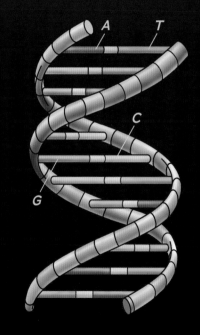

ABOVE: *About 2 inches (5 centimeters) long, this golden lace nudibranch* (Halgerda terramtuentis) *is from the Northwestern Hawaiian Islands. DNA bar coding will help show how closely it's related to other kinds of nudibranchs.*
RIGHT: *Samples for DNA bar coding were taken from this file clam collected by scientists on Australia's western reefs during the Census.*

Open Water

It's unnerving, not seeing the bottom. You can't see anything, in fact, except water tinted in different shades of blue. Above, the seawater is a bright, brilliant blue. It's lit by shafts of sunlight streaming down from the surface. Looking outward, the water is a rich medium blue, like the best blue crayon in the box. The water below is a deeper, darker blue that seems to go on forever. Far from shores and coral reefs, you're out in the open ocean in the Celebes Sea, in the western Pacific Ocean.

"Blue-water diving is a little like floating in outer space, except the space is all a beautiful blue instead of black."

—Larry Madin,
Woods Hole Oceanographic
Institution, Massachusetts

Blue-water divers hang weightless in the open ocean. A system of safety lines, attached to a small boat at the surface, keeps the divers from drifting away.

Journey
into the
deep

There's a gentle tug at your waist. It's your safety line. The other blue-water divers in the water around you are tethered in the same way. A glance at your dive computer shows that you're using the air in your tank pretty fast. Calm down. Breathe slowly. Try to find what the scientists on this Census expedition are looking for: the nearly invisible animals that make up an incredible floating zoo. As a group, they're called zooplankton. They drift with the current, like you're doing right now.

You stare at the blue water until your eyes hurt. Where are they? Suddenly something catches the light an arm's length away. It's definitely alive. But its body is almost clear. And it has . . . wings. You carefully remove a jar from the mesh bag hanging from your waist and unscrew the lid. Moving in slow motion, you gently trap the delicate creature inside.

Now that you know what to look for, you see other zooplankton in the water around you. You drift along in pursuit.

Scientists collected many kinds of sea butterflies on the Census. These marine snails have fleshy parts that they use like wings to "fly" through the water. Many have pointy, transparent shells like this one and are no bigger than a kernel of popcorn.

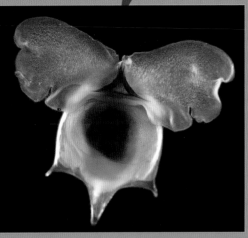

Having eyes on stalks helps this baby squid spot danger coming from any direction. Many kinds of squids spend the first weeks of their lives floating and feeding near the ocean's surface.

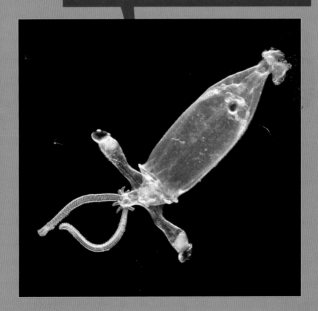

Measuring about 1.6 inches (4 centimeters) across, this rare siphonophore is a cousin of jellyfish. It moves through the open water by waving the clear, petal-like parts that surround the colored center of its body.

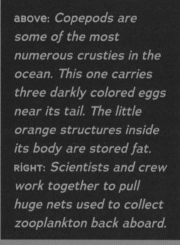

ABOVE: *Copepods are some of the most numerous crusties in the ocean. This one carries three darkly colored eggs near its tail. The little orange structures inside its body are stored fat.*
RIGHT: *Scientists and crew work together to pull huge nets used to collect zooplankton back aboard.*

Back on the ship, scientists carefully transfer the animals you and the other divers have caught to aquariums in the ship's lab. Before these zooplankton are preserved and bar-coded, the researchers will study and photograph them. It would be great to stay and watch the animals for a while. But that will have to wait.

Out on deck, the crew begins lowering an enormous net over the side of the ship. It's actually several nets stacked together. Each one can open independently underwater. This allows scientists to collect zooplankton at different depths, so they can figure out which species live where.

Nets work best for catching zooplankton that have hard, tough bodies. That's because strong currents swirl through the nets as they're pulled behind the ship. Those currents damage soft-bodied zooplankton trapped in the nets. But hard-bodied kinds can be captured unharmed.

Several hours later, you're helping haul the nets back on board. Many of the animals caught in the nets are crustaceans, relatives of crabs and shrimp. Most are smaller than the eraser on the end of a pencil.

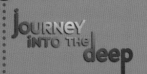

Just after dinner, a change in the rumble of the engines indicates the ship is slowing down. On the rear deck, crew members are preparing to launch the remotely operated underwater vehicle (ROV).

The ROV is the tool scientists will use to catch soft-bodied jellies that live far below the ocean's surface. The little underwater robot is linked to the ship by a bundle of cables, and it has cameras and containers for catching zooplankton.

A crane lifts the ROV over the side of the ship and into the water. Along with the scientists, you head for a big metal structure bolted to the deck. It has a door but no windows. Scientists call the structure the van. It's the control center for the ROV.

Inside, video screens cover one wall. The ROV pilot slides into his seat beneath them. He flips a few switches, and the screens flicker to life. Suddenly you're seeing what the ROV's cameras are seeing beneath the ship. The pilot gently grips the joystick that controls the ROV.

Lights! Cameras! Action! The ROV used by Census scientists in the Celebes Sea descends into deep water on its way to work. The four clear containers at the front can open and shut to trap small animals inside.

Bioluminescence

Bioluminescence is light produced by living things. If you've ever watched fireflies flash on summer nights, you've seen bioluminescence in action.

In the deep ocean, many animals are bioluminescent. Most produce light in special light organs. These light organs contain chemicals that, when mixed together, release energy as light. It's typically a blue green glow. Some bioluminescent jellyfish have light organs trimming the bottom edge of their bell. Many deep-sea fish have rows of light organs along the sides or undersides of their bodies.

Some deep-sea animals produce light to communicate with other members of their species. Some produce light to confuse predators. A few use it to lure a potential meal within striking distance. Almost all bioluminescent animals will flash when disturbed by another ocean creature—or an ROV!

A hush falls over the van as the ROV descends. Everyone's eyes are glued to the screens. The dark blue water gets darker by the second. The pilot turns on the ROV's lights. A depth recorder shows the ROV is 330 feet (100 meters) down. Soon it's 650 feet (198 meters), then 1,000 feet (305 meters). The water is so dark now, it's more black than blue.

Then the ROV's lights pick out an even darker shape. The pilot guides the sub closer. The dark shape is a fish, but it doesn't look like any type you've ever seen. For a few seconds, the fish hangs motionless in the water. Then, with a flick of its fins, it veers away from the ROV and is gone.

The ROV continues down, down, down. Every few seconds, tiny sparks flash on the video screens. They twinkle like stars in the night sky. A scientist explains that the flashes are coming from animals in the water around the ROV. Many animals in the deep ocean make their own light. It's called bioluminescence.

At about 1,640 feet (500 meters) down, a lacy, transparent something drifts past the ROV's cameras. It's definitely a comb jelly but a kind the scientists have never

During the years of the Census, scientists got a closer look at many unusual fish. The barreleye (Macropinna microstoma) is one of the most remarkable. It has a transparent head and huge eyes topped by dome-shaped, green lenses. The barreleye can roll its eyes in many directions—including backward to look straight up through the top of its head!

journey
iNTO THE
deep

seen before. The pilot moves the ROV closer. With the push of a button, the top of one of the containers on the front of the sub slides open. The pilot positions the container's wide mouth directly under the comb jelly. Seconds later, it's inside. The lid slides shut. The jelly is trapped.

Hours pass as the hunt continues. Another comb jelly is caught, and so is a tiny, bloodred jellyfish. Then, suddenly, an animal the scientists don't recognize at all appears on the video screens. The front half seems to have tentacles, like those of a squid. The back half looks like an ocean worm, with rows of bristly hairs.

The "squidworm" is soon settled inside the last container. The ROV begins the journey back to the surface. Soon you're helping carry the containers to the lab. There scientists gently release each animal into a small aquarium of its own.

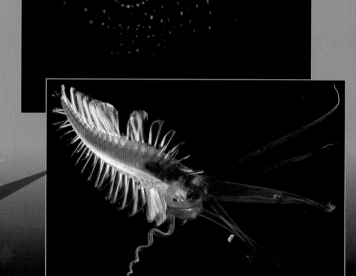

Bioluminescent spots glow on the underside of a small squid.

RIGHT: *The squidworm is a new species in a new family of marine worms. It is about 4 inches (10 centimeters) long and swims using the blue bristles along its body.*
BELOW: *Before the Census, no one had ever seen this deepwater comb jelly. The floppy projections, or lobes, on its body are covered with sticky mucus. It uses the lobes to catch small animals within reach.*

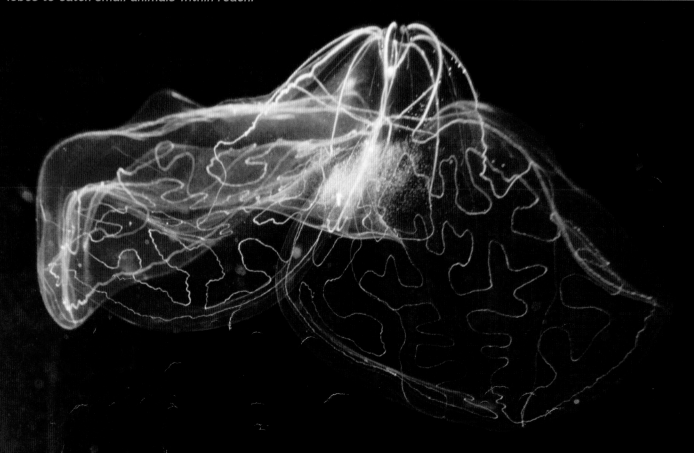

deep SLopes

PROPPED UP ON ONE ELBOW, YOU'RE LYING ON YOUR SIDE. YOUR NECK IS TWISTED. YOUR FOREHEAD IS PRESSED HARD AGAINST THE GLASS. YOUR MUSCLES ARE CRAMPING, AND YOU'RE GETTING COLD. BUT NONE OF THAT MATTERS. AS AMAZING AS IT WAS TO EXPLORE THE OCEAN WITH AN ROV, THIS IS BETTER. THIS IS THE REAL THING.

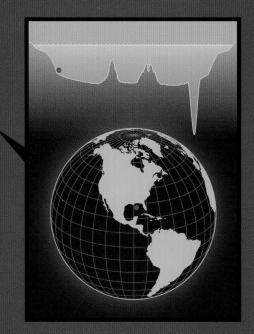

Scrunched inside a submersible that has just passed 1,476 feet (450 meters), you're descending through a dark world few people have seen. You stare out the small porthole, hardly daring to blink. Zooplankton drift and dart past the glass every few seconds. Many are bioluminescent.

Somewhere below is your destination. You're with a team of Census scientists who are studying a site on the continental slope of North America that stretches south into the Gulf of Mexico. Continental slopes are the submerged edges of continents. Some slant sharply down, forming steep cliffs. Others angle more gradually to the sea bottom.

Your headset crackles. From the forward compartment, the pilot announces that there's coral dead ahead. Where? You can't see anything but black water. Then the submersible turns so your porthole faces the slope.

A deep-sea coral reef, as it looks from a submersible's front compartment.

The sub's bright lights illuminate the scene. Outside is a pink coral as big as a tree. It's covered with electric blue worms.

The sub moves slowly along the slope, past a garden of deep-sea corals. They have formed a huge reef here, like their shallow-water cousins do near the ocean's surface. Yellow, pink, orange, red—the colors of the corals are amazing. Of course, if the pilot turned off the sub's lights, you wouldn't see anything at all. These corals grow in total darkness, in water that's just a few degrees above freezing.

How fast do deep-sea corals grow? The scientist sitting up with the pilot tells you that most species grow only 0.04 inches (1 millimeter) a year. Your fingernails grow that much in less than two weeks. Scientists have analyzed samples of deep-sea corals to estimate their age. Some are hundreds, even thousands, of years old. That makes these beautiful animals among the oldest living things on Earth.

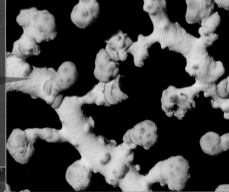

RIGHT: *Blue flatworms grip the bumpy pink branches of this bubblegum coral* (Paragorgia arborea).
BELOW: *The fragile, feathery branches of this deep-sea coral* (Iridogorgia pourtalesii) *grow in perfect spirals.* Iridogorgia *corals can reach at least 6.6 feet (2 meters) tall.*

WATER PRESSURE

It's not just cold and dark in the deep sea. The water pressure is also enormous. Water pressure is the force of water pressing in from all sides. The pressure increases the deeper you go.

In the ocean's top 3.3 feet (1 meter), for example, water presses in on something with a force of about 16 pounds per square inch (psi) (1.1 kilograms per square centimeter). At 328 feet (100 meters) down, the pressure is ten times that, or about 160 psi (11.3 kilograms per square centimeter). At 13,123 feet (4,000 meters)—the ocean's average depth—it's 5,846 psi (411 kilograms per square centimeter). If you were subjected to that kind of pressure, it would be like having a large pickup truck parked on every square inch of your skin.

Most animals in the deep sea have hard or rubbery bodies with no air spaces. Even under great pressure, they can't be crushed. When scientists bring these deep-sea creatures to the surface, the change in pressure doesn't affect them very much.

The sub moves slowly toward a clump of what the scientist says is bamboo coral. It has slender branches that divide again and again.

As the sub gets closer, the pilot turns out most of its lights. The sub has a mechanical arm that can collect things underwater. The pilot uses it to reach out and touch the coral. A soft blue glow flickers up and down its delicate branches. This bamboo coral is bioluminescent.

Next, you cruise over a massive patch of branching coral that's nearly as white as snow. The scientific name of this coral is *Lophelia pertusa*. It may be the most common reef-building deep-ocean coral in the world—or at least on the deep reefs that scientists have explored so far.

LEFT: *Slender bamboo corals grow among thick-stalked anemones.*
BELOW: *In this close-up of* Lophelia pertusa, *you can see the tiny, fleshy tentacles of the coral animals sticking out from the branches. They use these tentacles to snag bits of food from the water.*

"Every time we go to sea to study deep-sea corals we learn something new. Very few people even know these amazing coral communities exist."
—Erik Cordes, Temple University, Pennsylvania

Deep-sea coral reefs are home to many other kinds of living things. Almost every coral you see has at least one animal perching on it. Brittle stars and basket stars wind their long arms around and around coral branches. Long-legged squat lobsters and orange-headed shrimp hold on with pointed claws.

The sub's cameras flash, recording different scenes. The pilot uses the mechanical arm to collect small samples of several different corals and put them into containers mounted on the front of the sub. Then you're leaving, heading farther down the slope. The coral garden fades to black as the darkness engulfs it.

RIGHT: *Census scientists exploring a deep-sea reef in the Coral Sea, northeast of Australia, discovered this new species of blind lobster among the corals. They don't yet know how it uses its incredibly long, toothed pincer.*
BELOW: *A basket star grips its coral perch with many-branched arms.*

CHEMOSYNTHESIS

Plants, algae, and some microorganisms use energy from sunlight to turn water and the gas carbon dioxide into sugars that they use for food. This process is called photosynthesis. Living things that carry out photosynthesis form the first link in most of the food chains on Earth. Much of what you eat, for example, either comes from plants or something that eats plants.

In the deep ocean, where sunlight cannot reach, some food chains start with living things that carry out chemosynthesis. These organisms—mostly bacteria—use chemicals such as methane as an energy source for making their own food. Some animals living around cold seeps survive by keeping chemosynthetic bacteria in their bodies and sharing the food the bacteria make. Others live by eating the bacteria directly.

Farther down the continental slope, bubbles start fizzing past the porthole. For one terrifying moment, you're sure the submersible is leaking air. The scientist calmly explains that you've arrived at a cold seep, a place where gases are bubbling up from the seabed. The gases are methane and hydrogen sulfide. If you could smell the water outside the submersible, it would stink like rotten eggs.

Microscopic bacteria use these stinky gases as a source of energy in a food-making process called chemosynthesis. Billions of chemosynthetic bacteria live around cold seeps. What look like patches of white stuff on the seafloor are actually dense clusters of these bacteria.

Studying life around cold seeps was an important part of the Census of Marine Life. Teams of scientists explored these little-known communities of life along continental slopes worldwide, where bubbles of gas come fizzing out of the seabed.

"LIFE IS EVERYWHERE IN THE DEEP SEA. BUT WHERE THERE IS METHANE, THERE ARE TRULY EXPLOSIONS OF LIFE."

—*Lénaïck Menot, Institut Océanographique/ French Research Institute for Exploitation of the Sea (Ifremer), France*

JOURNEY INTO THE deep

From the porthole, you spot what looks like a bush growing up from the seafloor. But as the sub gets closer, it's obvious that this is no shrub. It's a cluster of spindly, red-topped tube worms.

The worms have no mouth or stomach. Tucked inside their long bodies are special organs packed with bacteria. The worms take in chemicals from the water and the seafloor that the bacteria need for chemosynthesis. The bacteria use them to make food for themselves and their worm hosts.

Fist-sized mussels huddle in groups near the tube worms. Chemosynthetic bacteria live inside their bodies too.

RIGHT: *Tube worms* (Lamellibrachia luymesi) *at a cold seep extend their feathery tops into the dark water. The rest of a tube worm's body is protected by a tough, flexible tube that's made of a substance similar to your fingernails. On one dive in 2002, scientists used a harmless dye to stain the tubes of these worms blue. On a second visit, in 2003, they measured the length of the tubes above the blue stain as a way to estimate how fast the worms grow. Tube worms like these may live to be as much as two hundred years old.*
BELOW: *Deep-sea mussels cling to bacteria-covered rocks near a cold seep. Blind shrimp rest among them.*

Several minutes later, and deeper still, the submersible glides over what looks like a small, dark lake. Thousands of mussels surround it, crowding right up to the edge. These are similar to the bacteria-hosting mussels you saw at the cold seep. The fact that the mussels are here is a sign that the area around the lake is rich in methane.

The pilot says the lake itself is a brine pool. The dark water is four or five times saltier than ocean water. Being so salty, it's much denser and heavier than seawater. The salty water has settled into a low spot here on the seabed.

The water in the brine pool is too salty for the mussels. That's why they live around but not in it.

LEFT: *A submersible cruises over a brine pool in the Gulf of Mexico. The supersalty water is so dense that the sub can float on top of the pool without sinking in. Scientists exploring in submersibles have found other deep-sea brine pools, including one that's nearly 12 miles (20 kilometers) long.*
BELOW: *Countless mussels live around the edge of a brine pool.*

The submersible has been exploring for almost three hours. There's time for one last stop before it must return to the surface. In the glare of the lights, you soon see a rocky overhang coated with what looks like orange sherbet. It's actually frozen methane.

At depths below about 1,970 feet (600 meters), the water pressure is so great that methane gas freezes as it comes out of the seabed, forming methane ice. Here the orange ice is covered with dozens of little hollowed-out spots. Nestled in each one is a slithery pink worm. The worms have a row of bristles on each side of their bodies. The bristles are moving, but the ice worms are not. They look as if they're all running in place.

Methane ice worms (Hesiocaeca methanicola), each about 1 to 2 inches (2.5 to 5 centimeters) long, sit in the depressions they've carved out for themselves in a solid chunk of orange methane ice.

"Ice worms graze on bacteria that live on the ice. The way the worms move creates water currents that bring oxygen to the bacteria and also makes the little pockets that they live in."

—Charles Fisher, Pennsylvania State University

the dark zone

Stepping out on deck, you snug up the zipper of your insulated coveralls. The bitterly cold wind feels as if it's coming straight down from the North Pole. It's hard to believe this is summer.

The grinding, squealing sound of breaking ice fills the morning air. At the front of the ship, the reinforced bow is plowing through the sea ice that forms a hard crust on the water's surface. Huge blocks of broken ice are shoved aside as the ship slowly steams forward. Ocean exploration is hard no matter where you are. But here in the Arctic Ocean, ice makes doing just about everything more difficult.

By midmorning, the ship has carved a wide path through the ice. Crew members lower the ROV into an area of open water. They use long poles to push aside a few ice chunks that threaten to drift too close to the cables that connect the sub to the ship. Minutes later, you're crowding into the van with the team of scientists studying

During the Census of Marine Life, many research teams traveled to both the Arctic and Southern oceans. Using ROVs like this one, they explored parts of these remote, ice-covered seas that had never been visited by scientists before.

life in these polar waters. Before the Census of Marine Life, few research expeditions had ever ventured this far north.

The pilot turns on the ROV's lights. She maneuvers the little sub up, down, and around to make sure all the controls are working perfectly. To test the camera, she sends the ROV out to a chunk of sea ice floating a short distance away. The camera focuses on the underside of the ice. It's covered with small crustaceans called amphipods. Amphipods are shrimp-like animals found pretty much everywhere in the ocean. One of the scientists says these amphipods are eating tiny algae that were trapped in the ice when it froze.

Testing complete, the ROV descends. On this dive, it's going deep—very deep. The scientists have many names for the vast realm of cold, dark water that lies below 3,280 feet (1,000 meters). Some call it the midnight or dark zone. For others, it's the abyss. By any name, it is a world far beyond the reach of even a single ray of sunlight.

Delicately jointed legs and antennae sprout from this 2.4-inch (6-centimeter) Arctic amphipod. Amphipods are an important food source for small fish and zooplankton such as comb jellies. Scientists discovered dozens of new types of these small crustaceans during the Census.

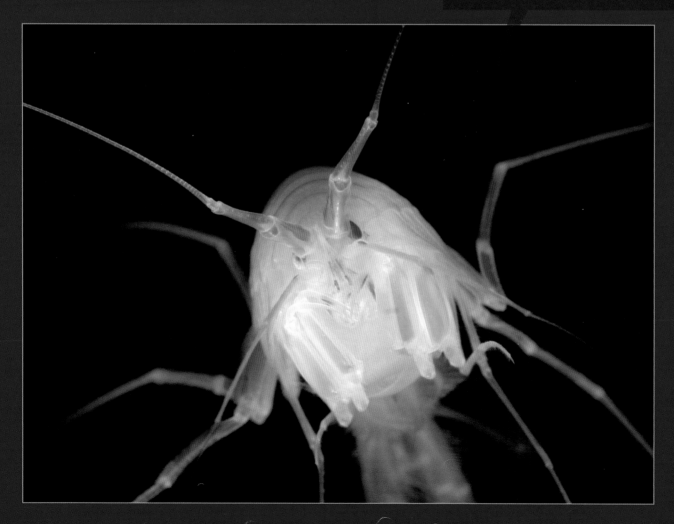

The ROV slowly descends into water that is jet black, sparkling now and then with bioluminescence. Deepwater fish dart past. You catch glimpses of sharp fangs. Food is scarce in the dark zone. Nearly everything is hunting something else.

At 3,937 feet (1,200 meters), the ROV's lights pick out something hanging motionless in the inky darkness. It's a siphonophore, a type of gelatinous zooplankton. The top half of this animal's body is made up of nearly transparent swimming bells, all attached to a sort of stem. Below the bells are long tentacles. Each is as fine as a hair and covered with stinging cells. A siphonophore hunts by spreading its tentacles to form a deadly net.

For a few minutes, the siphonophore seems to pose for the ROV's cameras. Then the bells at its top end begin to contract. With remarkable grace, the hunter swirls away like a kite on an invisible string.

Several hundred feet farther down, two very different jellyfish come into view. The jellyfish expert on the team squints at the screen. One is similar to a species he's seen before. The other might be new to science.

The pilot guides the ROV up to the first jellyfish. In less than a minute, it's corralled inside one of the sub's containers. The second jellyfish isn't so cooperative. Every time the ROV gets close, it moves just out of reach. As the minutes tick by, the pilot starts to sweat. No one says a word, for fear of breaking her concentration. When at last Jellyfish Two is safely inside a container, the van erupts with clapping and cheers.

ABOVE RIGHT: *A siphonophore (*Marrus orthocanna*) contracts its tentacles into a red orange mass beneath its swimming bells. When the tentacles are relaxed and stretched out, the entire animal is about 6.6 feet (2 meters) long.*

RIGHT: *A jellyfish about the size of a quarter pulses through the blackness of the abyss. Its stomach is the only part of its body that's not see-through. This allows the jellyfish to eat bioluminescent creatures and still remain invisible to other hunters in the water.*

Census scientists discovered this never-before-seen jellyfish in cold Arctic waters. It has four long tentacles for capturing food. The extremely short tentacles along the bottom of its transparent bell, however, are a puzzle. How the animal uses them or for what remains a mystery. This jellyfish is a new species in a new genus. Its scientific name is Bathykorus bouilloni.

"OFTEN WHEN I'M STUDYING JELLYFISH I FEEL LIKE I'M LOOKING AT A LIFE-FORM FROM ANOTHER PLANET. YET IN A SENSE, IT'S THEIR PLANET AND WE'RE THE ALIENS."

—Kevin Raskoff,
Monterey Peninsula College,
California

LEFT AND RIGHT: These two comb jellies are both new species discovered by Census scientists in the Arctic. Like all comb jellies, they move with the help of eight rows of tiny hairs that beat rhythmically like miniature oars. Both devour smaller zooplankton by sucking them into their gaping mouths. The one on the left would fit on your thumbnail. The one on the right is just a little bit bigger.

At 7,500 feet (2,286 meters) down, the ROV comes upon a large, plump comb jelly. It has two white tentacles that stick out like wild hairs. One of the scientists calls out that it's a very rare type that has been seen only a few times before in the deep sea. Its nickname is the Sunkist comb jelly because it's the size and color of an orange.

As the pilot maneuvers the sub closer, it brushes one of the comb jelly's tentacles. The tentacle sticks fast to the sub's metal frame. The pilot tries to shake the animal loose by moving the ROV from side to side through the water. The tentacle stays stuck. The pilot powers the sub backward. The tentacle stretches out like a giant rubber band. At last, it pulls free.

Five minutes later, the sticky comb jelly is safely inside a container. A bright orange worm becomes the final catch of the dive.

LEFT: *Scientists encountered this Sunkist comb jelly for the first time in the Arctic Ocean during the Census of Marine Life. Before that, this rare type, which belongs to the genus* Aulococtena, *had been seen only a few times before in deep waters off California and in the North Atlantic Ocean. Comb jellies with tentacles use them to catch smaller animals and stuff them into their mouths. Researchers had no idea what Sunkist comb jellies eat. But when this particular animal was brought to the surface, it spit out the remains of its last meal—a large, orange worm (BELOW) exactly like the one the scientists collected on the same ROV dive!*

The ROV's video camera is still on as the sub heads toward the surface. Suddenly a shadowy form glides in front of the lens. A large unblinking eye stares back at you from the deep. It's an eye very much like your own.

The deep-sea octopus hovers in front of the ROV. Its eyes roam over the sub and the containers mounted at the front. The octopus glides forward. It grips the containers with the tips of its tentacle-like arms. Is it trying to get at the animals inside?

The pilot moves the sub a little. Startled, the octopus abruptly lets go. It spreads its arms wide. You see for the first time that they are connected by skin, like webbing between a duck's toes. In one fluid movement, the octopus flares its arms backward and over its body. It holds this defensive pose for a few seconds. Then it turns right side out again, squeezes its arms together, and shoots away into the eternal night.

LEFT AND BELOW: *When turned inside out, the webbed arms of this deep-sea Dumbo octopus (*Stauroteuthis syrtensis*) completely cover the rest of its body. The small suckers on the undersides of its arms are bioluminescent. Census scientists encountered and collected a number of never-before-seen types of octopuses and squids in the Arctic and other parts of the ocean during their ten-year quest.*

"SQUIDS AND OCTOPODS HAVE COMPLEX BRAINS. THEIR INTELLIGENCE IS QUITE ADVANCED, BUT IT'S PROBABLY VERY DIFFERENT FROM OTHER ANIMALS THAT WE THINK OF AS INTELLIGENT."

—Mike Vecchione, National Oceanic and Atmospheric Administration/ Smithsonian Museum of Natural History, Washington, D.C.

aBYSSaL PLaiNS

Finally, the ocean is calm. The sun is out, and the wind has dropped to a gentle breeze. Yesterday a storm appeared on the horizon here in the middle of the Atlantic Ocean. The ship's crew and the science team worked as fast as they could. They bolted and strapped everything down. When the storm hit, the ship began to pitch and roll. The waves were huge. You'd heard people talk about how awful it feels to be seasick. You didn't believe them. Now you do.

Your stomach is still a bit queasy. In a few minutes, you'll be too busy to think about it, though. The trawl is coming up.

The trawl is a small net with a wide mouth attached by a strong cable to a winch on the deck. It took nearly two hours to lower the trawl down to the ocean floor. It dragged along the bottom for a few minutes, scooping up a sample of whatever's down there. Then the winch began reeling the cable back in.

When the trawl breaks the water's surface, crew members guide the net over the ship's rail. The net is choked with mud. Things are about to get messy.

Scientists begin the process of separating animals from mud hauled up from the bottom of the Arctic Ocean. During the Census, many hundreds of seafloor samples like this were collected from all the major ocean basins.

You help the science team scoop the mud into buckets. Soon you're covered with it. In the ship's laboratory, you begin separating animals from slimy ooze. The bigger animals are pretty easy to find. You uncover several sea stars and a couple of small sea cucumbers.

Next comes the job of separating out the tiny creatures. The first step is to spoon a bit of bottom mud into a sieve with small holes. Then you carefully flush the sample with water. The mud drains through the sieve's holes, leaving the living things behind. For every large animal on the ocean floor, there are thousands of little ones. They include nematode and polychaete worms, and all sorts of small bottom-dwelling amphipods and copepods. There are even minute bivalve (two-shelled) mollusks, relatives of much bigger clams and mussels.

Sorting through the mud takes most of the morning. You help preserve dozens of animals in alcohol. It will take Census scientists months, even years, to identify all of them, back in their laboratories on land.

Marine Snow

Mud on the ocean floor isn't like mud from a garden or a riverbank. It's largely made up of tiny particles of marine snow. The particles are all that's left of dead ocean organisms that once lived far above the bottom. Marine snow sinks slowly down through the water, like snowflakes. Eventually it becomes part of the bottom ooze.

RIGHT: *Shimmering like gold, this new type of copepod is a Census of Marine life discovery from the bottom of the Atlantic Ocean.*
BELOW: *Collected near Antarctica, this new species of amphipod sports a spiny covering on its 1-inch-long (2.5-centimeter) body.*

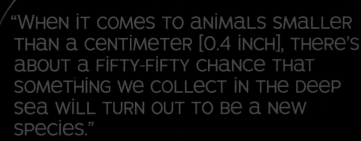

"WHEN IT COMES TO ANIMALS SMALLER THAN A CENTIMETER [0.4 INCH], THERE'S ABOUT A FIFTY-FIFTY CHANCE THAT SOMETHING WE COLLECT IN THE DEEP SEA WILL TURN OUT TO BE A NEW SPECIES."

—Pedro Martinez Arbizu, Senckenberg Research Institute and Natural History Museum, Germany

(3,048-meter) journey down has begun.

When the bottom finally comes into view, the submersible's bright lights reveal a landscape that's remarkably flat. More than half of the ocean bottom is like this, the scientist says. These great flat expanses of seafloor are called abyssal plains.

Hovering just above the bottom, the sub moves slowly forward. A half dozen sea cucumbers are the first life-forms you encounter. They look to be the same kind that the trawl brought up. The pudgy, fleshy creatures crawl across the seafloor, devouring mud as they go. The mud, with its amazing collection of tiny animals, bacteria, and other nutrients, is a source of food for many bottom dwellers.

LEFT: *This sea cucumber (*Scotoplanes globosa*) uses the tentacles around its mouth to pick up mud as it strolls across the ocean bottom. The long, antenna-like structures at both ends of its body may help it sense its surroundings in a pitch-black world.*
BELOW: *A sea urchin on the abyssal plain bristles with spines. They are needle-sharp and tipped with small white sacs of poison.*

"IN SOME PLACES THE SEA BOTTOM IS JUST CARPETED WITH SEA CUCUMBERS, THOUSANDS OF THEM."
—Bodil Bluhm, University of Alaska–Fairbanks

journey iNTO THE deep

Farther on, sea urchins sit like spiny gumdrops. They, too, are mud eaters. Their mouths are on the undersides of their dome-shaped bodies.

And then . . . nothing. The submersible passes over an area that appears to be empty of animals. Where the lights strike the ocean floor at just the right angle, though, you see odd tracks. The scientist thinks they were probably made by sea stars slithering across the soft surface.

A spiral of mud left on the bottom is also mysterious. It looks like toothpaste squeezed from a tube. A ten-minute search reveals one of the spiral makers in action. It's a worm-like animal with a bloodred body. It moves in an ever-widening circle as it eats. Mud goes in one end. Wastes pass out the other, leaving a distinct spiral signature.

LEFT: *In the Atlantic Ocean, a team of Census researchers photographed this remarkable red worm-like animal at a depth of about 7,545 feet (2,300 meters). They gave it the nickname spiral poo worm because of the unique droppings it leaves behind. Spiral poo worms can grow up to 3.3 feet (1 meter) long. When they finish eating in one spot, they rise up off the bottom, drift to a new location, and settle down to start eating again.*

BELOW: *Like sea cucumbers and sea urchins, sea stars on abyssal plains survive by eating mud. They move slowly across these flat landscapes on tiny tubular feet that sprout from the underside of each arm.*

The submersible moves slowly along through this extraordinary world. You never know what is going to appear next. Some of the animals the sub comes across are recognizable. But others are completely alien.

These deep-sea tunicates live with their bottom parts anchored in the ooze on the ocean floor. The top parts work like little pumps, moving water in one opening and out another, and filtering out bits of food in the process. Other animals perch on the tunicates, trying to improve their chances of catching a passing meal.

Most sponges pump water through their bodies to filter out food. A few rare deep-sea species, like this knee-high ping-pong tree sponge, are carnivorous. Any small crustacean or worm that touches one of the blue balls gets stuck. Cells in the balls surround and digest it. Several new species of carnivorous sponges were discovered on abyssal plains during the Census of Marine Life.

Tripod fish spend most of their time standing on the ocean bottom. They rest on three enormously long fins and wait for a meal to come along.

ABOVE: *This newly discovered see-through sea cucumber was creeping along on the seafloor when Census scientists spotted it. After a while, it spread fleshy parts of its body like wings and began to "fly" away. Its last meal of mud is visible inside its twisting stomach.*

LEFT: *Although they look like flowers, sea pens are animals that use their tentacles to catch food in the water just above the ocean bottom.*

39

Two hours into the dive, something very large appears on the ocean floor ahead. It's a collection of huge bones. A long-extinct dinosaur? The scientist smiles and shakes her head. It's a whale—or at least what's left of one.

A whale fall is what scientists call a dead whale that has sunk to the ocean floor. In life, this whale was one of the largest animals on Earth. In death, it is an enormous food supply. Its arrival has brought more food to this patch of ocean bottom than could fall as marine snow in four thousand years.

Deep-sea sharks, hagfish, and crabs are the first diners to arrive when a whale's body comes to rest on the seafloor. These animals devour the whale's skin, muscles, and other soft tissues. After a few months, the skeleton is all that's left.

A very different group of animals eats the bones. Most are quite small. But there are so many of them that they completely cover the skeleton. Some species are unique to whale falls. Scientists have yet to find them anywhere else.

The bone-eating zombie worm is one of these unique animals. Zombie worms have no mouth or stomach. They do have "roots" that grow deep into whale bones. The roots are packed with bacteria that break down fat inside the

Zombie worms belonging to the genus Osedax *(there are several species) all but cover the bones of a whale fall on deep abyssal plains. Herds of sea cucumbers feed on the ooze around the skeleton. A handful of pale squat lobsters clamber over the remains of the whale's skull.*

journey iNTO THe deep

bones. The bacteria convert the fat into a form that they and their worm hosts can use as food.

The submersible slowly circles the whale fall. The pilot uses the manipulator arm to collect a piece of bone that's packed with zombie worms. Then he announces that it's time to return to the surface and the ship. Moments later, the worm-covered skeleton vanishes into the darkness once more. It may lie there for another hundred years, giving life to one of the most unusual collections of animals on the planet.

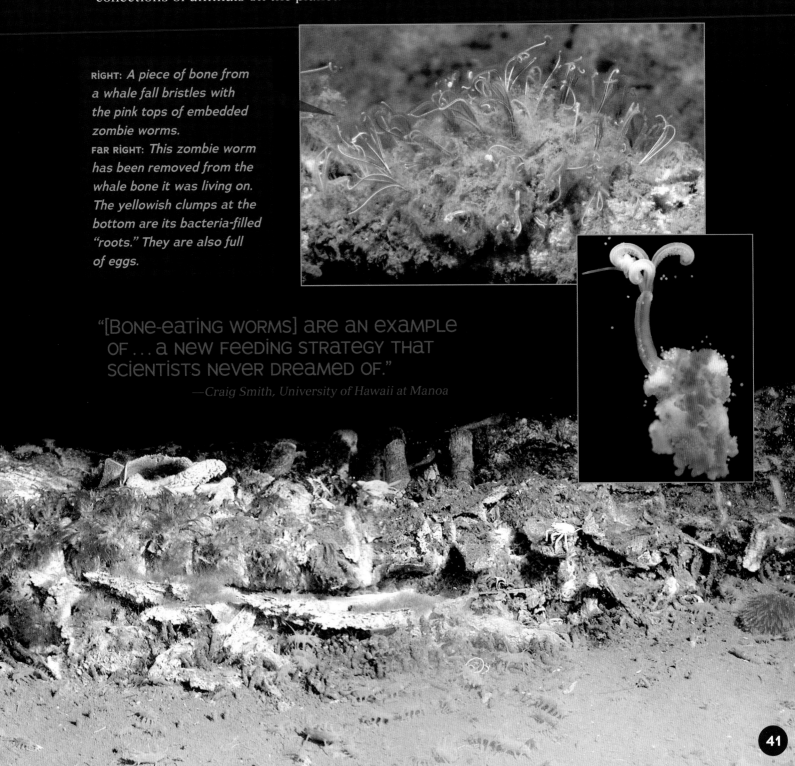

RIGHT: *A piece of bone from a whale fall bristles with the pink tops of embedded zombie worms.*
FAR RIGHT: *This zombie worm has been removed from the whale bone it was living on. The yellowish clumps at the bottom are its bacteria-filled "roots." They are also full of eggs.*

"[BONE-EATING WORMS] ARE AN EXAMPLE OF . . . A NEW FEEDING STRATEGY THAT SCIENTISTS NEVER DREAMED OF."
—*Craig Smith, University of Hawaii at Manoa*

mountains in the Sea

THE IMAGE OF A RAINBOW-COLORED MOUNTAIN FLICKERS TO LIFE ON THE COMPUTER SCREEN. BUT THIS IS NO ORDINARY MOUNTAIN. IT'S A SEAMOUNT, OFF NEW ZEALAND'S EASTERN COAST. SEAMOUNTS ARE CONE-SHAPED UNDERWATER MOUNTAINS THAT TOWER ABOVE THE SEAFLOOR. MOST ARE EXTINCT VOLCANOES. SOME SEAMOUNTS STAND ALONE ON ABYSSAL PLAINS. OTHERS FORM CLUSTERS OR CHAINS.

The Census scientists you're working with on this expedition are seamount experts. They've studied these ocean features all over the world. They won't need to travel far, though, to explore the seamount mapped on the computer screen. It's directly under the ship.

There's a good view of the rear deck through the window of the lab. Crew members are making minor adjustments to the ROV. You've got about fifteen minutes before the little sub is launched. That's enough time for a walk around the deck.

The wind has picked up in the past hour. Whitecaps dot the ocean's surface. Flocks of seabirds do too. Seabirds always seem to know where the fish are. They've come to the right place. Seamounts and the water around them are bursting with life.

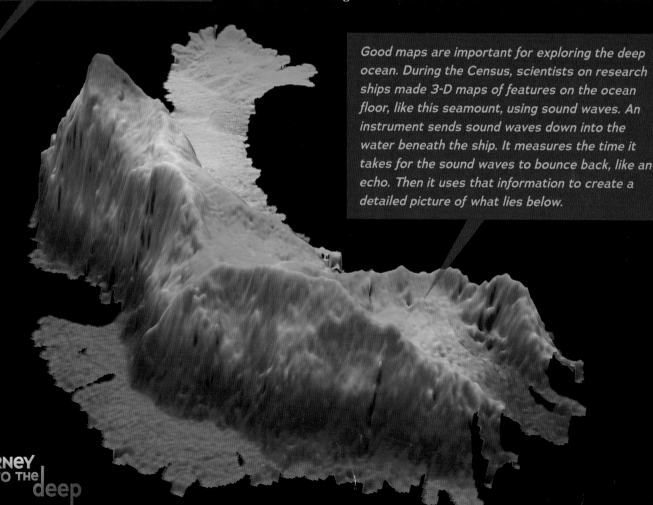

Good maps are important for exploring the deep ocean. During the Census, scientists on research ships made 3-D maps of features on the ocean floor, like this seamount, using sound waves. An instrument sends sound waves down into the water beneath the ship. It measures the time it takes for the sound waves to bounce back, like an echo. Then it uses that information to create a detailed picture of what lies below.

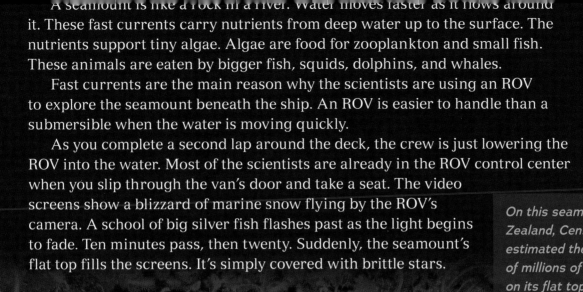

A seamount is like a rock in a river. Water moves faster as it flows around it. These fast currents carry nutrients from deep water up to the surface. The nutrients support tiny algae. Algae are food for zooplankton and small fish. These animals are eaten by bigger fish, squids, dolphins, and whales.

Fast currents are the main reason why the scientists are using an ROV to explore the seamount beneath the ship. An ROV is easier to handle than a submersible when the water is moving quickly.

As you complete a second lap around the deck, the crew is just lowering the ROV into the water. Most of the scientists are already in the ROV control center when you slip through the van's door and take a seat. The video screens show a blizzard of marine snow flying by the ROV's camera. A school of big silver fish flashes past as the light begins to fade. Ten minutes pass, then twenty. Suddenly, the seamount's flat top fills the screens. It's simply covered with brittle stars.

On this seamount near New Zealand, Census scientists estimated there were tens of millions of brittle stars on its flat top. They named it Brittle Star City.

For a few minutes, the ROV cruises over the mountaintop. Then the little sub nosedives over the edge and plummets down the seamount's steep sides. Enormous deep-sea corals project from jagged, rocky slopes. Their thick branches extend far out into the current where they can snare bits of food passing by.

You recognize some of the corals from your dive on the continental slope. Others are species you've never seen before. Scientists think that like islands, seamounts may be very different from one another. It's possible that some species live on just one seamount and nowhere else.

Big, brightly colored sponges sprout among the corals. Their rubbery bodies tremble in the current. They draw water in through countless holes and filter out whatever is good to eat.

Scientists call sponges like the one below Picasso sponges. Small pink shrimp and at least one squat lobster have made this boulder-size Picasso sponge their temporary home.

Several new types of Venus flytrap anemones were discovered on seamounts during the Census. When disturbed, some release bioluminescent slime.

"Very little is known about what actually lives on seamounts—only 300 to 400 have been sampled out of a possible global total close to 100,000."

—Malcolm Clark, National Institute of Water and Atmospheric Research, New Zealand

Many small animals such as squat lobsters take shelter among the corals and sponges. Others peek out from under rock ledges. They're hiding from the schools of hungry fish cruising past the steep slope. The scientists in the van call out the names of different species. Blue ling. Roundnose grenadier. Silver dory. Boar fish. Blue-eye trevalla. A burly orange roughy passes by inches from the ROV. Someone says it's probably more than one hundred years old. Like deep-sea corals, most deepwater fish grow very slowly.

The dive continues, but after a while, you notice that the video screens inside the van have begun to tilt from side to side. Of course, it's not the screens but the ship. Gradually, the tilting becomes a hard lurching. The captain appears in the doorway. The wind is whipping the ocean's surface into a churning mass of ragged, white-topped waves. The dive must be canceled. The ROV's cables could snap, and the little sub would be lost to the deep. Before the video screens go black, you catch a last view of the seamount and a huge, shimmering school of fish. Then everyone scrambles out onto the heaving deck to help get the ROV safely back on board.

A squat lobster perches on a clump of Lophelia pertusa *coral.*

Ridges and Vents

First, the ship sailed east. Then it sailed west. Now it's heading east again. You ask one of the scientists on this expedition to the southeastern Pacific Ocean what's going on. He explains that the ship is towing an instrument back and forth above the ocean floor. It's searching for signs of hydrothermal vents.

A hydrothermal vent is a place in the ocean floor where hot, chemical-rich water comes blasting out. The towed instrument is searching for traces of this vent water. Judging by the excited shouts that suddenly fill the air, it's just found some.

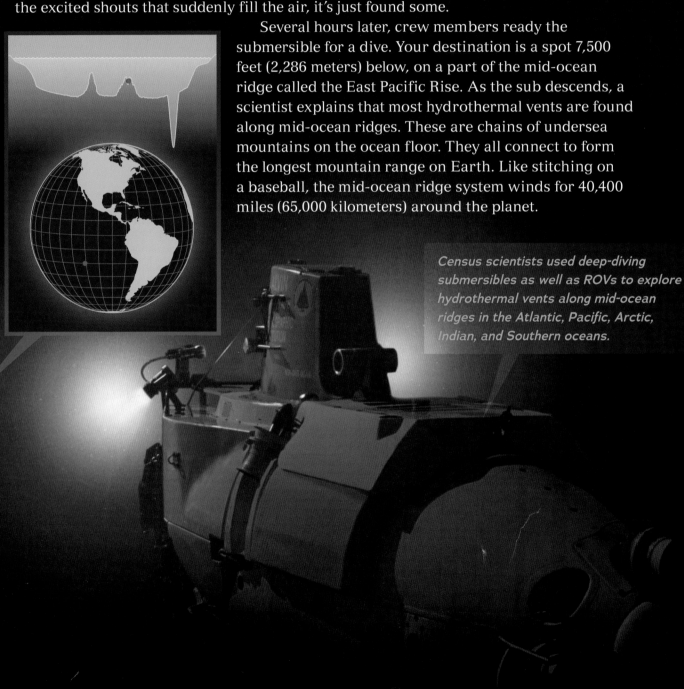

Several hours later, crew members ready the submersible for a dive. Your destination is a spot 7,500 feet (2,286 meters) below, on a part of the mid-ocean ridge called the East Pacific Rise. As the sub descends, a scientist explains that most hydrothermal vents are found along mid-ocean ridges. These are chains of undersea mountains on the ocean floor. They all connect to form the longest mountain range on Earth. Like stitching on a baseball, the mid-ocean ridge system winds for 40,400 miles (65,000 kilometers) around the planet.

Census scientists used deep-diving submersibles as well as ROVs to explore hydrothermal vents along mid-ocean ridges in the Atlantic, Pacific, Arctic, Indian, and Southern oceans.

Your first glimpse of the mid-ocean ridge is a surprise. There's no soft mud here. The submersible's lights pick out masses of barren volcanic rock. These rocks are new pieces of Earth's crust. They formed when magma, or melted rock, surged up through a crack in the ocean floor and cooled in the near-freezing water.

Slowly the submersible clears a jagged ridge. On the other side, jets of what looks like black smoke stream up from chimney-like vents among the rocks.

Black, blistering hot fluid erupts from a hydrothermal vent along a mid-ocean ridge. It's easy to see why scientists call vents like these black smokers.

MOVING PLATES

Earth's crust is made up of about two dozen gigantic rocky plates that fit together like pieces of a jigsaw puzzle. Mid-ocean ridges mark the places where these massive plates are slowly moving apart. Magma from beneath the crust comes up at these spreading plate boundaries. It cools to form new crust. In some areas, this new crust is riddled with hydrothermal vents, underwater geysers of dark, chemical-laden seawater that's as hot as 750°F (400°C)!

"MY FIRST DIVE TO A VENT SITE WAS IN THE FRENCH SUBMERSIBLE *NAUTILE*, ON THE MID-ATLANTIC RIDGE. TRAVELING DOWN THROUGH THE DARK WATER, I STARED AND STARED OUT THE TINY PORTHOLE. AND THEN SUDDENLY, THE BLACK SMOKERS WERE IN FRONT OF US."
—Eva Ramírez-Llodra, Institut de Ciències del Mar, Spain

Around the vents, giant tube worms—as tall as a person—grow in great clumps. The scientist wants to get a closer look at these strange animals. The pilot carefully guides the sub through a maze of black smokers. Passing directly over one would be a serious mistake. The dark fluid is hot enough to melt parts of the submersible. Outside, the water pressure is enormous. If the sub cracked, you'd be crushed in an instant.

After a few minutes of careful maneuvering, the sub is flanked by tube worms on both sides. Their feathery plumes sway just outside the portholes. Like their cousins at cold seeps, the worms harbor billions of chemosynthetic bacteria inside their bodies.

Chemosynthesis powers life around hydrothermal vents, just as it does at cold seeps. These giant tube worms (Riftia pachyptila) take up chemicals from the water through their fluffy, plumed tops. Chemosynthetic bacteria inside the worms turn the chemicals into food.

The tube worms share their space with other animals. Snail-like limpets the size of mini jelly beans are inching their way up the outsides of the tubes. Scuttling among them are pink worms covered with scales that overlap like shingles on a roof.

The sub moves out of the forest of tube worms and over a field of large mussels. They lie in heaps on the bottom, crowding out everything else. Ghostly white squat lobsters scurry over and around them.

This bright pink species of scale worm is often found living with giant tube worms at hydrothermal vents. New types of scale worms were discovered during the Census of Marine Life. Some of these worms obviously like it hot. They cluster near the tips of black smokers!

Mounds of mussels cluster so thickly at some hydrothermal vents that they completely obscure the ocean bottom.

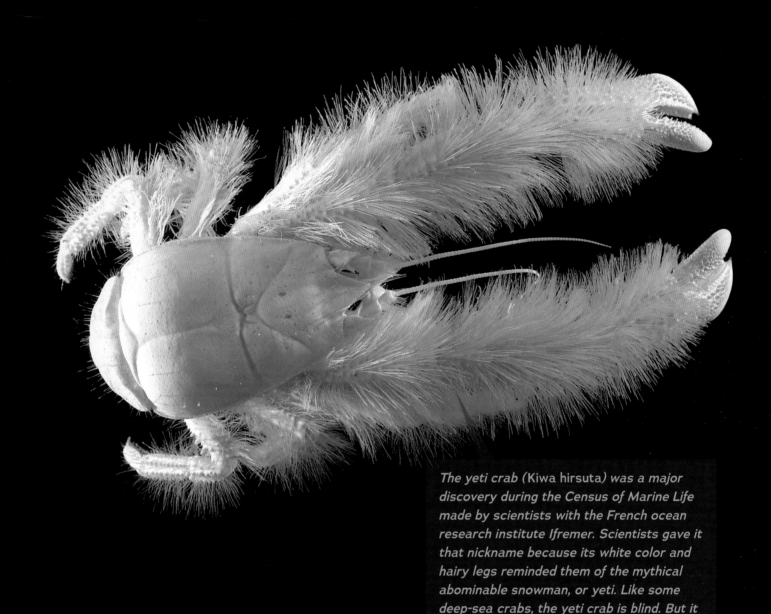

*The yeti crab (*Kiwa hirsuta*) was a major discovery during the Census of Marine Life made by scientists with the French ocean research institute Ifremer. Scientists gave it that nickname because its white color and hairy legs reminded them of the mythical abominable snowman, or yeti. Like some deep-sea crabs, the yeti crab is blind. But it is so different from other crab species that scientists created a new genus and a new family to classify it. The yeti crab in this picture is about as long as your hand.*

Something else that's white catches the pilot's eye. He eases the sub closer and lets out a triumphant cry. It's a yeti crab, a strange, newly discovered species with remarkably hairy legs.

Yeti crabs have only been found at a few vent sites. They may be rare, but scientists can't really say for sure. The reason is that no two vents are exactly alike, even in the same part of the ocean. They'll have many species in common. But they won't be identical.

What's even more puzzling are the differences scientists have found between vents in different ocean basins. Pacific Ocean vents like this one are home to giant tube worms, mussels, and clams. Vents in the Atlantic and Indian oceans swarm with blind shrimp.

Mid-ocean ridges are nearly continuous all the way around the world. So why don't vents in every ocean basin have pretty much the same collection of

animals? During the Census of Marine Life, scientists studied vents all over the world trying to answer that question. They still don't know.

Just as baffling is how new vent communities form. Tube worms and other animals that cannot move produce eggs that hatch into larvae. Larvae drift off in search of new vents where they can settle down and grow into adults. But how the larvae find the vents remains a mystery. Solving these deep-sea puzzles is an enormous challenge. Every dive to a hydrothermal vent, however, yields a few more clues.

When the time comes for the sub to ascend, it's hard to leave the vents behind. But you know you've just become a member of a small group of very lucky people who have seen them firsthand.

"HOW DO LARVAE FIND NEW VENTS? THAT'S THE MAIN QUESTION! THEY CANNOT ACTIVELY SWIM IN A PARTICULAR DIRECTION, ESPECIALLY AGAINST A CURRENT. AT THIS POINT, WE SIMPLY DO NOT KNOW HOW THEY DO IT."
—Paul Tyler, National Oceanography Centre, Southampton, United Kingdom

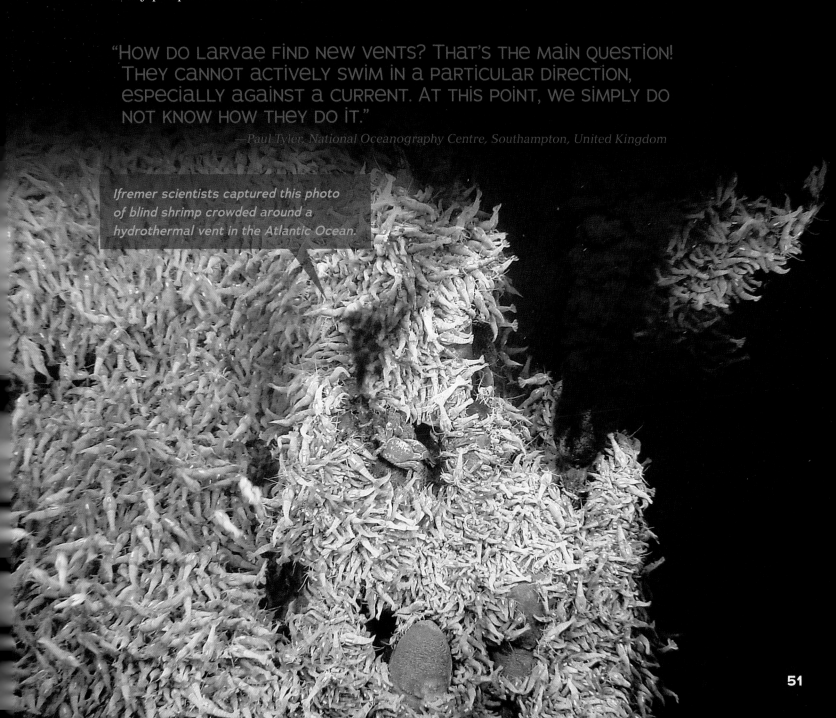

Ifremer scientists captured this photo of blind shrimp crowded around a hydrothermal vent in the Atlantic Ocean.

the UNFATHOMaBLe deep

COMPARED TO a SUBMERSIBLE, THE LANDER DOESN'T LOOK LIKE MUCH. IT HAS NO MECHANICAL ARMS OR CONTAINERS FOR COLLECTING ANIMALS. THERE ARE NO COMPARTMENTS AND NO THICK CABLES CONNECTING IT TO THE SHIP. IT'S JUST a METAL FRAME WITH a CAMERA IN THE MIDDLE. THAT FRAME, THOUGH, IS MADE OF TITANIUM, ONE OF THE STRONGEST METALS KNOWN. THE CAMERA LENSES ARE FORMED FROM a SUPERHARD CRYSTAL CALLED SAPPHIRE. THE LANDER IS INCREDIBLY TOUGH. IT HAS TO BE TO DESCEND TO THE BOTTOM OF THE JaPaN TRENCH HERE IN THE NORTHERN PaCIFIC OCEaN.

Trenches are the ocean's deepest places. They form where plates making up Earth's crust slide under other plates. Trenches range from about 16,400 feet (5,000 meters) to roughly 36,000 feet (almost 11,000 meters) deep. That's nearly 7 miles (11.3 kilometers) below the surface. The water pressure at the ocean's deepest point is so great it would be like having fifty jumbo jets piled on top of you.

Carefully, scientists and crew lower the lander into the water. It's heavily weighted. When it's released, the lander sinks like a stone. Even so, it will take five hours for it to reach the bottom of the Japan Trench. Once there, its camera will turn on and start to take pictures of whatever's down there, in that unfathomably deep place.

Two days later, everyone is standing at the ship's rail, staring down into the water. About five hours ago, the scientists sent a signal down to the lander. The signal triggered the release of the weights. The lander started the long journey back to the surface.

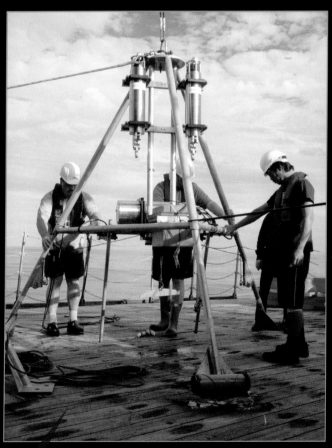

52

Simple and strong, the lander is built to withstand the immense pressure found in the ocean's deepest places— and the free-falling descent to get there. Its camera is positioned in the center, protected by the three long legs.

A cheer goes up as the lander breaks the surface. Soon it's out of the water and sitting safely on the deck. The scientists don't see any obvious damage. Its camera looks intact. ·

In the lab, what the camera recorded comes to life on a video screen. The video shows a group of ghostly pale snailfish. They are swimming and eating—at 25,272 feet, or 4.8 miles (7,703 meters) below the ocean's surface. Fish have been brought up in trawls from such depths before. But they're dead by the time they reach the surface. They can't survive the tremendous pressure change. You're watching history in the making. These are the deepest living fish that have ever been captured on film.

"NOBODY HAS SEEN FISH ALIVE BEFORE AT THESE DEPTHS—ONLY PICKLED [PRESERVED] IN MUSEUMS."
—Monty Priede, University of Aberdeen, Scotland

ABOVE: Many "firsts" occurred during the Census of Marine Life, including the filming of these snailfish (Pseudoliparis amblystomopsis) at the bottom of the Japan Trench.
ABOVE RIGHT: Deep-sea snailfish are well-suited for life at extreme depths. They have rubbery, crushproof bodies covered with gelatinous skin. A keen sense of smell, "feelers," and other special sensory structures help them locate food in utter darkness

explore the ocean firsthand? Then think seriously about becoming an ocean scientist. You can start right now by studying biology and math in school. Learn as much as you can about the ocean and ocean life from library books and on the Internet. Visit an ocean aquarium, and talk to the people who work there. Many ocean scientists and conservation groups have blogs about research, issues, and current events. Get online and join the conversation.

(7,217 meters) down. They had thought it was impossible for fragile zooplankton to survive at such depths. This comb jelly proved them wrong. And it's not just a new species. It's unlike any comb jelly ever seen before.

This new type of comb jelly—the deepest living comb jelly known—uses string-like structures to anchor itself to the seafloor. Two tentacles stream out behind its body, ready to capture anything that blunders into them.

The Mariana Trench in the Pacific is the ocean's deepest trench. The lowest point in that trench, roughly 35,761 feet or 6.8 miles (10,900 meters) down, is a place called the Challenger Deep. Two very special ROVs, built to survive extreme depths, have visited the Challenger Deep. They've returned with samples of ocean floor ooze. In the samples, researchers found small animals and other life-forms, including one-celled creatures called foraminifera. At least four of these foraminifera are types that are new to science.

It seems that every part of the ocean—no matter how cold or dark or deep— is home to some type of life. On your journey with Census scientists, you've seen many weird and wonderful living things. But as you head back to land, the inevitable question remains: what else is out there, still waiting to be discovered? Perhaps one day in the not-too-distant future, you'll be part of another ocean census that will be working hard to find out.

"WHEN YOU PICK UP AN ANIMAL AND REALIZE THAT WHAT YOU ARE LOOKING AT IS SOMETHING NO ONE ELSE HAS EVER SEEN— A SPECIES THAT AS YET HAS NO NAME—IT'S HUMBLING AND ALSO QUITE THRILLING."
—Joel (Jody) Martin, Natural History Museum of Los Angeles County, California

The nearly transparent skin of this deep-dwelling, swimming sea cucumber (Enypniastes eximia) is studded with bioluminescent dots. When attacked, it can shed its glowing skin and glide away unnoticed into the darkness. How much time these sea cucumbers spend swimming versus feeding on the ocean bottom is one of many things scientists have yet to discover about them.

epilogue

For the ten years of the Census of Marine Life, scientists explored cold polar waters and warm tropical seas. They investigated what lives at the ocean's surface, on its bottom, and in everything in between. Their hard work has helped create a much clearer picture of what lives in the ocean worldwide.

All along the way, Census scientists discovered amazing new life-forms. At the time this book was published, they had identified approximately 5,600 new species. The final count will probably be closer to 10,000 when all the preserved samples have been examined by experts. That would raise the number of known and named ocean species to more than 250,000. That's a lot. Yet some Census scientists think millions more ocean species still await discovery.

Discovering new species was an exciting and important part of the Census. But just as important was what scientists learned about biodiversity and how ocean life is distributed worldwide. There were many surprises. For example, hundreds of identical species live in both Arctic and Antarctic waters, even though these regions are separated by 6,835 miles (11,000 kilometers). Far more kinds of animals live in ocean floor ooze than on it. Life in that deep-sea mud is as diverse as a tropical rain forest. Even seawater itself is bursting with life. In some places, just about 1 quart (1 liter) can contain twenty thousand different kinds of minute, one-celled living things.

Census scientists also discovered that certain types of jellies and other zooplankton are rare in some places and amazingly abundant in others. Cold seeps are much more common than anyone ever imagined—there's even one in the Japan Trench! Seeps also are home to many species that have not been observed anywhere else on Earth. Continental slopes, once thought to be barren wastelands, are absolutely teeming with life.

Colonies, or groups, of one-celled ocean organisms called radiolarians drift in the open water. The small white balls are individual radiolarians. The large, nearly transparent spheres are made up of fine strands that hold the members of the colony together.

Many are the sites of deep-sea coral reefs so vast that they dwarf most tropical, shallow-water reefs. And hydrothermal vents, together with their strange communities of life, are found along mid-ocean ridges worldwide.

The vast amounts of information Census scientists have gathered are being collected into huge databases. When complete, these databases will contain almost everything that is currently known about the ocean's living things. That knowledge is critical for what happens next.

The ocean faces many threats. Growing cities are consuming coastlines. Pollution and runoff from land are killing coral reefs. Many beaches and large areas of open ocean are choked with trash. Overfishing is pushing many fish species to extinction. In just a few hours, bottom trawls—huge heavy nets dragged for hours along the ocean floor to catch fish and other animals—can destroy a forest of deep-sea corals that took centuries to grow.

Another threat is global warming. Over the past few decades, human activities have added huge amounts of carbon dioxide and other gases to the atmosphere. These gases trap heat near the Earth's surface, raising temperatures on land and in the ocean. Carbon dioxide in the air also mixes into seawater, where it forms acid. Ocean warming is already harming tropical coral reefs. Ocean acidification is harming clams, snails, sea butterflies—anything with a shell. How these changes will affect other ocean life is unknown.

ABOVE: *A healthy deep-sea reef is home to fish, corals, brittle stars, anemones, and many other animals.*
BELOW: *Trawling has turned this reef into a lifeless jumble of broken, dead coral.*

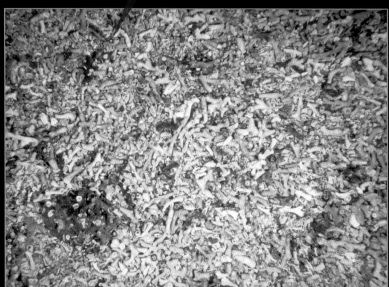

Protecting the Ocean

Protecting the ocean may seem like something only scientists and politicians can do. But everyone, including you, can make a difference. Saving energy may be the most important step you can take. Much of the world's electricity comes from burning coal, oil, and other fossil fuels. The carbon dioxide released in the process contributes hugely to global warming. Become an advocate for clean energy, such as solar and wind power.

Support groups that work to protect coastlines. Healthy, trash-free coastlines go a long way in protecting ocean species that live offshore.

Choosing not to eat fish can help reduce overfishing. If you must eat fish, choose kinds that are still abundant and are caught by methods that don't harm other types of ocean creatures. You can find information on ocean-friendly fish choices at http://www.edf.org/page.cfm?tagID=1521.

Learn as much as you can about ocean life, what threatens it, and ways to protect it. Share what you learn with others.

These are large and complicated problems. What scientists learned during the Census of Marine Life is an important step in solving them. It is a starting point for reversing some of the damage and protecting the ocean in the years to come.

Marine protected areas are one sign of progress. Since the Census began in 2000, many countries have created new marine protected areas or expanded existing ones. Marine protected areas help strengthen ocean biodiversity. They offer safe havens for many species. They give damaged ecosystems a chance to recover. Even so, only about 0.6 percent of the ocean has been protected in this way. Much more needs to be done.

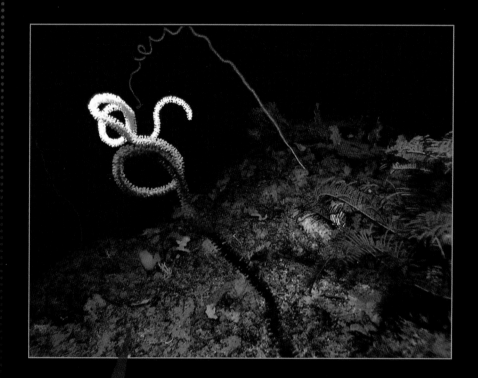

Delicate, coiling bamboo corals grow on a seamount in the North Atlantic Ocean. In 2009 scientists and environmentalists proposed making a 23,000-square-mile (59,570-square-kilometer) protected area around Atlantic deep-sea coral reefs off the eastern coast of the United States. Norway, Australia, Canada, New Zealand, and several other countries have created or are working to create similar protected areas.

The first Census of Marine Life began with scientists asking questions. How many species? Where do they live? How do they survive where they live? Asking questions—and finding answers—is what science is all about.

The search for answers will keep ocean scientists busy for a long time to come. They'll be studying shorelines, diving on coral reefs, setting sail for the open ocean, and exploring its vast and mysterious depths. As scientists carry out this important work, there's little doubt they will discover many more new wonders along the way.

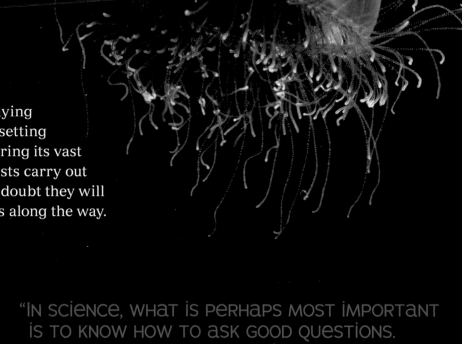

"IN SCIENCE, WHAT IS PERHAPS MOST IMPORTANT IS TO KNOW HOW TO ASK GOOD QUESTIONS. ONCE YOU KNOW THE QUESTIONS, YOU CAN GO ABOUT TRYING TO ANSWER THEM."

—Myriam Sibuet, Institut Océanographique, Paris, France

ABOVE RIGHT: *Rainbows of light from the camera's flash reflect off the bell of this deep-sea jellyfish* (Vampyrocrossota childressi)*. Barely bigger than a shirt button, it is the only known jellyfish that is truly black.* **ABOVE:** *An active swimmer, this ocean worm releases a bioluminescent fluid from the tips of its paddle-like "legs."* **RIGHT:** *Scientists think these delicate animals are the larvae of some type of deep-dwelling sea urchin.*

SCIENTISTS QUOTED IN THIS BOOK

 **Bodil Bluhm,** University of Alaska–Fairbanks

 **Ann Bucklin,** University of Connecticut

Charles Fisher, Pennsylvania State University

 **Erik Cordes,** Temple University, Pennsylvania

 **Joel (Jody) Martin,** Natural History Museum of Los Angeles County, California

Larry Madin, Woods Hole Oceanographic Institution, Massachusetts

 **Nancy Knowlton,** National Museum of Natural History, Smithsonian Institution, Washington, D.C.

 **Lénaïck Menot,** Institut Océanographique/ French Research Institute for Exploitation of the Sea (Ifremer), France

 **Pedro Martinez Arbizu,** Senckenberg Research Institute and Natural History Museum, Germany

 **Monty Priede,** University of Aberdeen, Scotland

 **Eva Ramirez-Llodra,** Institut de Ciències del Mar, Spain

 **Kevin Raskoff,** Monterey Peninsula College, California

 **Malcolm Clark,** National Institute of Water and Atmospheric Research, New Zealand

 **Myriam Sibuet,** Institut Océanographique, Paris, France

 **Paul Tyler,** National Oceanography Centre, Southampton, United Kingdom

 **Craig Smith,** University of Hawaii at Manoa

 **Mike Vecchione,** National Oceanic and Atmospheric Administration/ Smithsonian Museum of Natural History, Washington, D.C.

 **Boris Worm,** Dalhousie University, Nova Scotia, Canada

glossary

abyssal (uh-BIH-suhl) plains: immense, flat or gently sloping expanses of the deep ocean bottom, typically below a depth of about 9,843 feet (3,000 meters)

acidification (ah-sid-ih-fuh-KAY-shun): the process through which something such as ocean water comes to contain more acid

algae (AL-jee): plant-like living things that use energy from sunlight to make their own food. Some algae are very small and single-celled. Others are multi-celled and, like kelp and other seaweeds, can be large.

anemone: an ocean animal with stinging tentacles; tube anemones live in tubes; sea anemones attach their bottom ends to a surface

biodiversity: the variety of life in a place

bioluminescence (BYE-oh-LOO-mih-NESS-uhnts): light made by living things

census: a systematic counting and recording of everyone or everything that lives in a place

chemosynthesis (kee-moh-SIN-thuh-sis): a process where living things use energy from chemicals to make their own food

cold seep: a deep-sea ecosystem, often found on and near the base of continental slopes, where methane and other gases bubble or seep up from the seabed and life is largely supported by chemosynthesis; also called a methane seep

comb jelly: a gelatinous-bodied animal, related to jellyfish, that moves with the help of eight rows of beating hairs; also known as a ctenophore

continental slope: the sloping or steep margins of continents that are underwater. Continental slopes extend from the edge of the continental shelf to the ocean bottom.

coral reef: a structure found in warm, shallow, tropical ocean waters that is built by coral animals and home to an incredible variety of other living things. Deep-sea, cold-water corals also form reefs on continental slopes, seamounts, and parts of the ocean floor.

crustaceans (kruh-STAY-shunz): a general name for many kinds of invertebrate (no backbone) animals that have a hard or tough body covering. These include lobsters, crabs, copepods, amphipods, and shrimp.

deoxyribonucleic acid (dee-ahk-see-RYE-boh-nu-KLEE-ihk A-sid) (DNA): the substance in cells that carries information for building and maintaining a living thing; genetic material

ecosystem: a community of different kinds of organisms all living together in a particular place

foraminifera (fohr-am-uh-NIF-er-uh): amoeba-like single-celled organisms (protists) that have a shell or build a protective covering out of grains of sand or similar materials. Just one is a foraminifer.

global positioning system (GPS): a device that is used to find the exact position of something on Earth

global warming: the recent increase in Earth's average surface temperature, shown to be largely caused by human activities including the burning of oil, coal, and other fossil fuels

hydrogen sulfide (HY-druh-gin SUL-fyd): a colorless gas that has a foul smell, like rotten eggs

hydrothermal vent: an opening in Earth's crust, especially near mid-ocean ridges, from which superheated, chemical-rich water spews out; the source of chemicals that support deep-sea hydrothermal vent ecosystems

lander: an unmanned device for exploring extremely deep parts of the ocean that is not connected to a ship at the surface

larvae (lahr-VEE): small forms of a living thing that hatch from eggs and later change into the adult form. Just one is a larva.

marine snow: tiny bits of waste material that drift down through ocean water; a source of food for many ocean animals

methane (METH-ayn): a colorless gas, sometimes known as natural gas

mollusk (MAH-lusk): an animal belonging to a large group that includes snails, mussels, limpets, clams, squids, octopuses, and many others; sometimes spelled mollusc

nutrients: substances necessary for life

ocean basins: large expanses of ocean floor usually bounded by continents, for example the Pacific Ocean basin

seamount: an underwater mountain that rises from the ocean bottom but does not reach the ocean's surface

species: a unique type of living thing

specimen (SPEH-sih-men): an individual that is an example of a type or group

submersible: a small submarine vehicle used to explore the ocean. A manned submersible carries people inside.

trenches: in the ocean, the deepest features on the ocean floor

tropical: having to do with an area near the equator, where temperatures are warm year-round

whale fall: the body of a dead whale that has sunk to the ocean bottom; usually includes the communities of living things that obtain nutrients from the whale's tissues and bones

zooplankton (ZOH-oh-PLANK-tuhn): small animals that drift through ocean waters. Some are weak swimmers.

Source Notes

6 Boris Worm, quoted at Plenary Session, Census of Marine Life synthesis workshops, Long Beach, CA, February 5, 2009.

10 Nancy Knowlton, quoted at DNA bar-coding group session, Census of Marine Life synthesis workshops, Long Beach, CA, February 5, 2009.

14 Larry Madin, e-mail to author, March 17, 2009.

16 Ann Bucklin, interview with the author, Census of Marine Life synthesis workshops, Long Beach, CA, February 2, 2009.

22 Erik Cordes, e-mail to author, March 7, 2009.

24 Lénaïck Menot, e-mail to author, April 17, 2009.

27 Charles Fisher, e-mail to author, March 17, 2009.

31 Kevin Raskoff, telephone interview with the author, March 20, 2009.

33 Mike Vecchione, interview with the author, Census of Marine Life synthesis workshops, Long Beach, CA, February 5, 2009.

35 Pedro Martinez Arbizu, e-mail to author, May 6, 2009.

36 Bodil Bluhm, interview with the author, Census of Marine Life synthesis workshops, Long Beach, California, February 3, 2009.

41 Craig Smith, quoted in Graham Lawton, "Long Dark Teatime of the Zombie Worms," *New Scientist*, November 12, 2005, p. 51.

44 Malcolm Clark, Census of Marine Life, Census Conversations, n.d., http://www.coml.org/conversations/clark (March 29, 2009).

47 Eva Ramirez-Llodra, e-mail to author, January 16, 2009.

51 Paul Tyler, e-mail to author, December 19, 2008.

53 Monty Priede, quoted in Rebecca Morelle, "'Deepest Ever' Living Fish Filmed," BBC News online, October 7, 2008, http://news.bbc.co.uk/2/hi/science/nature/7655358.stm (March 29, 2009).

55 Joel (Jody) Martin, e-mail to author, February 23, 2009.

59 Myriam Sibuet, interview with the author, Census of Marine Life synthesis workshops, Long Beach, CA, February 4, 2009.

Selected Bibliography

Books

Crist, Darlene Trew, Gail Scowcroft, and James M. Harding Jr. *World Ocean Census: A Global Survey of Marine Life.* Buffalo: Firefly Books, 2009.

Ellis, Richard. *Singing Whales and Giant Squid: The Discovery of Marine Life.* Guilford, CT: Lyons Press, 2006.

Nouvian, Claire. *The Deep: The Extraordinary Creatures of the Abyss.* Chicago: University of Chicago Press, 2007.

Van Dover, Cindy Lee. *Deep-Ocean Journeys: Discovering New Life at the Bottom of the Sea.* Cambridge, MA: Perseus Publishing, 1996.

Websites

Arctic Ocean Diversity. http://www.arcodiv.org/index.html (March 31, 2009).

"Big Red Jelly Surprises Scientists." Monterey Bay Aquarium Research Institute. May 5, 2003. http://www.mbari.org/news/news_releases/2003/nr03-matsumoto.html (March 31, 2009).

Census of Marine Life. http://www.coml.org/ (March 31, 2009).

Census of Marine Zooplankton. http://www.cmarz.org/ (March 31, 2009).

Census of the Diversity of Abyssal Marine Life. http://www.cedamar.org (January, 2010).

Chemosynthetic Ecosystem Science. http://www.noc.soton.ac.uk/chess/ (March 31, 2009).

Monterey Bay Aquarium Research Institute. http://www.mbari.org/ (March 31, 2009).

"A Mystery Is Solved." Mar-Eco. March 29, 2005. http://www.mar-eco.no/mareco_news/2005/a_mystery_is_solved (March 31, 2009).

Ocean Explorer (NOAA). http://oceanexplorer.noaa.gov/welcome.html (March 31, 2009).

Woods Hole Oceanographic Institution Online Expeditions. http://www.whoi.edu/page.do?pid=8881 (March 31, 2009).

Learn More

Websites

Australian Institute of Marine Science
http://www.aims.gov.au/creefs/latest-field-trip.html
Read daily dispatches about scientific research on Australian tropical coral reefs during the Census.

Census of Marine Life
http://coml.org
This is the official website for the Census of Marine Life. Explore it to learn about all the different COML projects, discoveries, updates, and much more.

ChEss (Chemosynthetic Ecosystem Science)
http://www.noc.soton.ac.uk/chess/education/edu_home.php
Learn about deep-sea animal communities at hydrothermal vents, cold seeps, and whale falls at this COML project site.

COMARGE (Continental Margin Ecosystems)
http://www.ifremer.fr/comarge/en/Gallery_Biozaire.html
Explore a cold seep off the west coast of Africa in pictures and video.

Dive and Discover
http://www.divediscover.whoi.edu/
Join scientists from Woods Hole Oceanographic Institution on expeditions to different parts of the ocean, see photos and videos, and read interviews and scientists' logs about life at sea.

Marine Conservation Biology Institute
http://www.marineconservationblog.blogspot.com/
Check out the articles and comments posted on this ocean conservation group's blog.

MarineBio Conservation Society
http://marinebio.org
This group's website is packed with information about ocean life. Find out what others are saying about ocean issues or make your voice heard at their MarineBio Blog (http://marinebio.org/blog/).

NOAA (National Oceanic and Atmospheric Administration), Ocean Explorer
http://oceanexplorer.noaa.gov/
Check out photo and video highlights, read about recent expeditions, and take part in an ocean challenge puzzle.

Prepare to Descend
http://www.ocean.udel.edu/deepsea/home/home.html
Enjoy a digital dive into the deep sea at this information-packed website and test your ocean IQ.

Books

Baker, Maria. *Deeper Than Light*. Bergen, Norway: Bergen Museum Press, 2007. An international team of scientists involved in the COML wrote this book about exploring the deep ocean.

Earle, Sylvia A., and Linda K. Glover. *Ocean: An Illustrated Atlas*. Washington, DC: National Geographic, 2008. Maps, photos, and satellite images provide unique views of oceans and ocean life.

Johnson, Rebecca L. *A Journey into the Ocean*. Minneapolis: Carolrhoda Books, 2004. Follow a young sea turtle's ocean journey, visiting different marine ecosystems along the way.

Lindop, Laurie. *Venturing the Deep Sea*. Minneapolis: Twenty-First Century Books, 2006.

Learn more about submersibles, ROVs, and other tools scientists use to explore the sea.

Nouvian, Claire. *The Deep: The Extraordinary Creatures of the Abyss*. Chicago: University of Chicago Press, 2008. Close-ups of many deep-sea animals fill the pages of this book, along with personal essays from scientists.

Turner, Pamela S. *Prowling the Seas: Exploring the Hidden World of Ocean Predators*. New York: Walker & Company, 2009. This book highlights a COML project that involved tagging sharks, tuna, sea turtles, and other ocean predators to learn more about their habits and long-distance journeys.

Wojahn, Rebecca Hogue, and Donald Wojahn. *A Coral Reef Food Chain: A Who-Eats-What Adventure in the Caribbean Sea*. Minneapolis: Lerner Publications Company, 2010. Learn more about the animals that inhabit tropical coral reefs and who eats what.

Videos and DVDs

The Blue Planet. Seas of Life. Part 2: Open Ocean/The Deep. DVD. Directed by Alastair Fothergill. Burbank, CA: Warner Home Video, 2002. The BBC's acclaimed nature series takes viewers from surface water to abyssal plains and trenches.

Volcanoes of the Deep Sea. DVD. Directed by Stephen Low. Chatsworth, CA: Image Entertainment, 2005. Explore life around hydrothermal vents miles beneath the ocean's surface.

INDEX

abyssal plains, 36, 38, 42
acidification, ocean, 57
algae, 8, 9, 24, 29; as food, 43
amphipods, 29, 35
anemones, 2, 22, 44; Venus flytrap, 44
Antarctic waters, 6, 56
Arbizu, Pedro Martinez, 35, 60
Arctic waters, 28–29, 34, 56
Aureophycus aleuticus, 9

bacteria, 24, 25, 27, 41, 48
bamboo coral, 22, 58
barreleye fish (*Macropinna microstoma*), 18
basket stars, 23
Bathykorus bouilloni, 31
Big Red jellyfish (*Tiburonia granrojo*),
   4–5, 7
biodiversity, 6, 10, 56
bioluminescence, 4, 18, 19, 22, 30, 33,
   44, 55
black smokers. *See* hydrothermal vents
Bluhm, Bodil, 36, 60
brine pools, 26
brittle stars, 23, 43
Bucklin, Ann, 16, 60

Census of Marine Life, 4, 6–7;
   accomplishments of, 53, 54, 56–57
chemosynthesis, 24, 25, 48
Clark, Malcolm, 44
coastlines, 9, 57; protection of, 58
cold seeps, 24, 56
comb jellies (ctenophores), 2, 18–19,
   29, 31, 32, 54; deepest living, 54;
   Sunkist, 32
continental slopes, 20, 24, 56
copepods, 16, 35
coral reefs: age of, 21, 57; deep-sea,
   20–23, 56–57; environmental threats
   to, 57; shallow water, 10–12
corals, 4, 10, 21, 22, 44, 45, 57; bamboo,
   22, 58; bubblegum, 21; soft, 10
Cordes, Erik, 22, 60
crabs, 11; yeti, 50
Crossota novegica, 65
crustaceans (crusties), 16, 29, 38. *See
   also* amphipods
ctenophores. *See* comb jellies

depth chart, 7
DNA, 13
Dumbo octopuses, 2; *Stauroteuthis
   syrtensis*, 33

Earth, crust of, 47, 52
East Pacific Rise, 46
Enypniastes eximia, 55
environmental challenges, 57–58

Fisher, Charles, 27, 60
fishes, 6, 18, 39, 43, 45; barreleye, 18;
   flatfish, 4; ice fish, 6; snailfish, 53;
   tripod fish, 39; yellow boxfish, 2
food and feeding, 24, 25, 27, 29, 30,
   31, 32, 36, 37, 38, 39, 43, 44, 53, 54;
   bone eaters, 40–41; meat eaters, 38,

40; mud eaters, 36–37, 39; whale fall,
   40–41
foraminifera, 55

gases, undersea, 24
global warming, 57, 58
golden lace nudibranch (*Halgerda
   terramtuentis*), 12
Gulf of Mexico, 26

Halgerda terramtuentis, 12
Hesiocaeca methanicola, 27
hydrogen sulfide, 24
hydrothermal vents, 46–47, 57;
   temperature of, 47; worms near, 49

ice worms (*Hesiocaeca methanicola*),
   27
Iridogorgia pourtalesii, 21

Japan Trench, 52, 56
jellies, 2, 4–5, 15, 16, 17, 18–19, 29,
   30–32, 54, 56, 59, 65
jellyfishes, 4, 5, 14, 18, 30, 31; Big Red,
   4–5, 7; deep-sea, 59, 65

kelp (*Aureophycus aleuticus*), 9
Kiwa hirsuta, 50
Knowlton, Nancy, 10, 60

Lamellibrachia luymesi, 25
lander, 52–53
larvae, 51, 59
light organs. *See* bioluminescence
lobsters, squat, 11, 23, 40, 45, 49
Lophelia pertusa, 22, 45

Macropinna microstoma, 18
Madin, Larry, 14, 60
maps and mapmaking, 42
Mariana Trench, 55
marine snow, 35, 40
Marrus orthocanna, 30
Martin, Joel (Jody), 55, 60
Menot, Lénaïck, 24, 60
methane, 24, 25, 26; frozen, 27
mid-ocean ridges, 46–47, 50–51, 57
mud, deep-sea, 35, 55, 56; scientists
   sift, 34–35
mussels, 25, 26, 49

oceans: depth chart of, 7; protection
   of, 58; size and locations of, 5, 28;
   temperature of, 57; water pressure
   in, 21, 27, 48, 52
octopuses, 2, 12, 33; Dumbo, 2, 33;
   pygmy, 12
Osedax, 40
overfishing, damage from, 58

Pacific Ocean, 46
Paragorgia arborea, 21
Piccard, Jacques, 4
ping-pong tree sponge, 38
pollution, 57, 58
Priede, Monty, 53, 60
Pseudoliparis amblystomopsis, 53

radiolarians, 56
Ramirez-Llodra, Eva, 47, 60
Raskoff, Kevin, 31, 60
remotely operated underwater vehicle
   (ROV), 17–19, 28–29, 30, 31, 32, 43;
   limitations of, 45, 52
Riftia pachyptila, 48–49

Sakaila wanawana, 11
saltwater, density of, 26
scientific classification, 7, 13
Scotoplanes globosa, 36
scuba diving, 4, 10–11, 14–15
sea cucumbers (*Scotoplanes globosa*),
   35, 36, 39, 40; deep-dwelling, 55
seamounts, 42–44, 46, 58
sea pens, 39
sea stars, 4, 35, 37
sea urchins, 36, 37, 59
shrimps, 11, 23, 25, 51
Sibuet, Myriam, 59, 60
siphonophores, 15; *Marrus orthocanna*,
   30
Smith, Craig, 41, 60
snailfish (*Pseudoliparis amblystomopsis*), 53
snails, 11, 15; sea butterflies, 15
species, 6, 7; newly discovered, 7, 9,
   11, 12, 19, 23, 31, 35, 38, 44, 49, 50,
   56; number of, in ocean, 4, 56
sponges, 38, 44
squat lobsters, 45, 49
squids, 15, 33
squidworm, 19
Stauroteuthis syrtensis, 33
submersibles, 4, 20, 22, 23, 26, 36, 41,
   46, 48, 52

Tiburonia granrojo, 4, 7
trawls, 34, 36; bottom, 57
trenches, 52, 55, 56; deepest, 55; depth
   and water pressure of, 52
Trieste, 4
tube worms: *Lamellibrachia luymesi*
   25; *Riftia pachyptila*, 48–49
tunicates, 38
Tyler, Paul, 51, 60

Vampyrocrossota childressi, 59
Vecchione, Mike, 60
volcanoes, undersea, 42, 47

Walsh, Don, 4
water pressure, 21, 27, 48, 52
whale fall, 40–41
Worm, Boris, 60
worms, 11, 19, 21, 25, 27, 32, 35, 37, 48–49,
   59; ice, 27; reproduction of, 51; spiral
   poo, 37; tube, 25, 48–49; zombie, 40–41

yellow boxfish, 2
yeti crab (*Kiwa hirsuta*), 50

zombie worms (*Osedax*), 40–41
zooplankton, 14–17, 20, 30, 31, 56; diet
   of, 43; gelatinous, 2, 4–5, 15, 16, 17,
   18–19, 29, 30–32, 54, 56, 59, 65

PHOTO ACKNOWLEDGMENTS

The images in this book are used with the permission of: © Russ Hopcroft/UAF, front endsheets (sea butterfly), (copepod with eggs), pp. 15 (top right, bottom right), 16 (top left), back endsheets (baby squid); © Cory Pittman 2006/seaslugsofhawaii.com, front endsheet (sea slug), p. 13 (top); © 2002 MBARI, pp. 5 (right), front endsheets (big red jellyfish); © Kevin Raskoff, front endsheets (round comb jelly, long bioluminous siphonophore); pp. 29; 30 (both); 31 (all); 32 (both); p. 60 (right, third from bottom); 64 (bottom); back endsheets (arctic amphipod, horned combed jelly, Bathykorus bouilloni, Sunkist comb jelly); © Dr Julian Finn, Museum Victoria, front endsheets (pygmy octopus), p. 12 (bottom); Stefano Schiaparelli, NZ IPY-CAML Voyage, 2008; back endsheets (spiny amphipod), p. 35 (left); © Jeff Rotman/Digital Vision/Getty Images, (background) pp.1, 4, 65; Cheryl Clarke-Hopcroft/University of Alaska Fairbanks (UAF), p. 1; © Steven Haddock/ 2005 MBARI, p. 2; © David Shale/naturepl.com, p. 3 (top); © Michael Aw, pp. 3 (bottom); 14, 17, 19 (center), 55; © Macduff Everton/Terra/Corbis, p. 4 (left); © 2002 MBARI, p. 4 (right), 5 (bottom), 40-41 (bottom); NOAA/ Monterey Bay Aquarium Research Institute, pp. 5 (left, center), 21 (top), 36 (right), 44 (top); © Julian Gutt/Alfred Wegener Institute for Polar and Marine Research, p. 6; © Laura Westlund/ Independent Picture Service, pp. 7, 8 (top), 10 (top), 13 (right), 14 (top), 20 (top), 28 (top), 34 (top), 42 (top), 46 (top left), 52 (left); Photo by Tohru Iseto/ NaGISA 2008, p. 8; © Max Hoberg, p. 9 (top); © Jerry and Marcy Monkman/ DanitaDelimont.com, p. 9 (bottom); © Gary Cranitch/Queensland Museum, p. 10, 11 (right), 12 (top), 13 (bottom left); © Dr. Jody Martin/The Natural History Museum of Los Angeles County, pp. 11 (left), 60 (center, second from top); © Larry Madin/Woods Hole Oceanographic Institution, pp. 15 (left), 19 (bottom), 39 (top), 56; © PH Wiebe, Woods Hole Oceanographic Institution, p. 16 (right); © 2004 MBARI, p. 18; © Steven Haddock, http://lifesci.ucsb.edu/~biolum/, pp. 19 (top), 59 (all); courtesy of NOAA/Dr. Steve Ross, UNC-W. NOAA Office of Ocean Exploration., p. 20; Courtesy of NOAA/ Aquapix and Expedition to the Deep Slope 2007, p. 21 (bottom); © Erik Cordes and the Lophelia II: Reefs, Rigs, and Wrecks project/NOAA, p. 22 (top); Photo courtesy of Lophelia II 2009: Deepwater Coral Expedition: Reefs, Rigs, and Wrecks/NOAA, p. 22 (bottom); © Tin-yam Chan, National Taiwan Ocean University, Keelung, p. 23 (top); NURC/ UNCW and NOAA/FGBNMS, pp. 23 (bottom), 37 (right); © Ian MacDonald pp. 24, 26 (bottom), 27; © Erik Cordes/ Reefs Rigs and Wrecks Expedition and seaview systems inc/NOAA, p. 25 (bottom); © Charles Fisher, p. 25 (top); Courtesy of NOAA/OER, p. 26 (top); Courtesy of Jeremy Potter NOAA/OAR/ OER, p. 28; © David Shale/ DeepSeaPhotography.com, p. 33 (both); Courtesy of NOAA/Hidden Ocean 2005 expedition: NOAA Office of Ocean Exploration: p. 34; © Marco Buntzow/ Senckenberg Research Institute, p. 35 (right); © 2005 MBARI, p. 36 (left); © MAR-ECO, Institute of Marine Research, Norway, p. 37 (left); © Martin Riddle/Australian Antarctic Division, p. 38 (top); © 2003 MBARI, pp. 38 (bottom), 41 (top); © 2001 MBARI, p. 39 (top left); © David Wrobel/Visuals Unlimited, p. 39 (bottom left); © The Natural History Museum, London, p. 41 (inset, center right); © Larry Mayer/Center for Coastal and Ocean Mapping/NOAA-UNH Joint Hydrographic Center University of New Hampshire, p.42 (bottom) ; NIWA, © 2008, p. 43; © 2006 NOAA/MBARI, p. 44 (bottom); © Dr. Kenneth J. Sulak/ USGS, p. 45; ©David Batson/ DeepSeaPhotography.com, pp. 46, 49; The Stephen Low Company / Rutgers University/shot from the Alvin for IMAX film Volcanoes of the Deep Sea, p. 47; Images courtesy of Fisheries and Oceans Canada, pp. 48, 57 (both); Pacific Ring of Fire 2004 Expedition. NOAA Office of Ocean Exploration; Dr. Bob Embley, NOAA PMEL, Chief Scientist, p. 49 (bottom); © Ifremer / A. Fifis, p. 50; © Ifremer/French Research Institute for Exploitation of the Sea/ Victor-Exomar, p. 51; © Oceanlab University of Aberdeen, pp. 52, 53 (bottom); Image courtesy of NOAA/ Bodil Bluhm, University Alaska Fairbanks (UAF) and Ian MacDonald A&M University, Corpus Christi, p. 53 (top); © Dhugal John Lindsay, Ph.D., (JAMSTEC), p. 54; Courtesy of NOAA/ Voyage To Inner Space-Exploring the Seas, p. 58; courtesy of Bodil Bluhm, p. 60 (top left); courtesy of Ann Bucklin, p. 60 (top center); courtesy of Charles Fisher, p. 60 (top right); courtesy of Erik Cordes/ © Peter Batson, p. 60 (left, second from top); courtesy of Larry Madin, p. 60 (right, second from top); courtesy of Nancy Knowlton/National Museum of Natural History, Smithsonian Institution, p. 60 (left, third from top); courtesy of Leniack Menot/Ifremer, p. 60 (center, third from bottom); courtesy of Seckenberg Research Institute/© Torben Riehl, p. 60 (right, third from top); courtesy of Professor Imants (Monty) G. Priede, p. 60 (left, third from bottom); courtesy of Eva Ramirez-Llodra, p. 60 (center, third from bottom); courtesy of Malcolm Clark, p. 60 (left, second from bottom); courtesy of Myriam Sibuet, p. 60 (center, second from bottom); courtesy of Paul Tyler, p. 60 (right, second from bottom); courtesy of Craig Smith, p. 60 (bottom left); courtesy of Mike Vecchione, p. 60 (center bottom); courtesy of Boris Worm, p. 61 (bottom right); © Greg Rouse, back endsheets (zombie worm).

Front jacket cover: (new species, phylum Ctenophora) © Steven Haddock/ Monterey Bay Aquarium Research Institute; (ocean background) © Jeff Rotman/Digital Vision/Getty Images; front jacket flap: (*Grimpoteuthis* sp.) © 1999 Monterey Bay Aquarium Research Institute; back cover: (new species, class Polychaeta) © Michael Aw; author photo on back jacket flap: © Ann Hawthorne.

This deepwater jellyfish (Crossota norvegica) *was photographed during a Census of Marine Life expedition to the Arctic Ocean.*